COUNSEL
YOURSELF
& OTHERS
FROM THE
BIBLE

COUNSEL YOURSELF & OTHERS

FROM THE

BIBLE

The First Place to Turn for
Life's Tough Issues

.

BOB MOOREHEAD

MULTNOMAH BOOKS

COUNSEL YOURSELF AND OTHERS
FROM THE BIBLE
published by Multnomah Books
a part of the Questar publishing family

© 1994 by Dr. Bob Moorehead

International Standard Book Number: 0-88070-636-8
Cover design by David Carlson
Printed in the United States of America

Unless noted otherwise,
Scripture quotations are from the *New International Version*
© 1973, 1984 by International Bible Society
used by permission of Zondervan Publishing House

Also quoted:
The *New American Standard Bible*
© 1960, 1977 by the Lockman Foundation; used by permission

The *International Children's Bible, New Century Version*
©1986, 1988 by Word Publishing; used by permission

The Living Bible © 1971 by Tyndale House Publishers

The *King James Version*

For information:
Questar Publishers, Inc.
Post Office Box 1720
Sisters, Oregon 97759

Library of Congress Cataloging-in-Publication Data:

94 95 96 97 98 99 00 01 02 — 10 9 8 7 6 5 4 3 2 1

Publisher's Note

As suggested by its title, *Counsel Yourself and Others from the Bible* has been designed to help you dig into God's Word for the reliable guidance you need when dealing with life's toughest issues. However, while this book does encourage you to consult the Bible first, it is not the intent of the author or publishing team to suggest that further counseling may not be appropriate, effective, or even necessary in any given case.

God reveals His wisdom through a vast number of resources, including the thousands of godly men and women who work as Christian counselors. We should not underestimate the value of this resource; rather, we should use it intelligently, taking full advantage of such wise counsel when it is called for.

If you are facing a personal crisis, the most important action you can take is to ask for God's guidance in prayer. It is also important that you turn to the Scriptures for teachings that can help you in dealing with the issues at hand. If you feel it is God's will for you to obtain further counseling, make an appointment for a consultation with a Christian counselor. (See page 272 for tips on "How to Choose a Counselor.")

IMPORTANT: If the situation is potentially life-threatening to you or to any other person, or if you feel that you are experiencing a dangerous emotional crisis, feel free to seek additional counselors who know and trust God. You should not bypass the steps of prayer and Scripture examination. However, it is critical that you do not delay in getting the additional help you may need.

No matter what issues you face or how you resolve them, we pray that *Counsel Yourself and Others from the Bible* will prove to be a powerful tool in helping you successfully tap into the most effective, life-impacting wisdom available to you: the teachings in God's Word.

This book is dedicated to
the light of my life,
the encourager of my ministry,
and the queen of my house—
Glenita, my wife.

Table of Contents

Introduction

. . . . .

Jack, a muscular man in his late twenties, showed up at my office unannounced. My secretary looked ashen white as she told me, "I know he doesn't have an appointment, but I think you need to see him for a minute."

That minute turned into almost two hours. Jack had worked at the same job for the past decade. His salary was high, and as far as he knew, he had job security for years to come. But that day, he'd been fired by his boss.

"I'll get him, you wait! I'll get him!" Jack shouted as he pounded his fist on my desk. I had never seen a man so angry in all my life. After he paced around my office and vented his anger for about ten minutes, I was able to take Jack to several Scripture verses about crisis, anger, forgiveness, trust, and judgment.

For well over an hour, Jack and I prayed and read, prayed and read. We finally turned to Ephesians 4:26, which says, "In your anger, do not sin." Jack looked startled and said, "What does that mean, 'in your anger'?" I explained to him that the Bible does not forbid anger, but tells us to properly harness it.

Jack's eyes softened, and he actually managed a momentary smile. "You mean it's okay to get angry as long as I don't sin with it?" I assured him that was exactly right. I then showed him an important warning in Scripture: If we allow our anger to fester into bitterness, we are opening up a door for Satan to really thrash us.

Jack broke, began to cry, then realized that all his life he had handled conflict with an out-of-control approach. Not only did he write his boss a letter that day, he also ordered flowers for his boss and his wife. What a breakthrough! Was it me? No, it was the power of God's Spirit applying His Word in Jack's heart that had made this difference.

From that day on, I've been profoundly convinced that God's answers to our confusion are right before us, in His Word! No, Jack didn't get his job back, because the company was "downsizing"—cutting staff in the hope of becoming more efficient. But he was able to walk away with his head high, with no regrets, and, most importantly, with no animosity. Oh, the power of God's Word!

Elementary? Presumptuous? Too simplistic? Some (certainly not all!) in the soul and mental care fields would say, "It's too dangerous to tell troubled people something so simple as, 'Pick up your Bible and read it if you have problems.'"

Let me say at the outset that this book in no way is intended to discourage anyone from seeking additional help as they walk through dark and dangerous valleys in their lives. I praise God for those men and women of God who, skilled in applying the Word of God, counsel others and pray for them.

But this book strongly encourages anyone and everyone going through rough and troubling times to turn to God's Word *first*. It is written out of some very strong convictions about the Bible, God's infallible Word. Let me give you a brief rundown of some of these convictions:

1. The Bible is fully inspired and authoritative.

It is the authoritative and inerrant Word of God. It is "God-breathed."

All Scripture is God-breathed and is useful for teaching, rebuking, correcting and training in righteousness, so that the man of God may be thoroughly equipped for every good work (2 Timothy 3:16-17).

Scripture is not the words of men, it's the Word of God. Being the Word of God, it is flawless in content. There is no error or mistake in it. King David boldly declared, "the words of the Lord are flawless" (Psalm 12:6). Later in life, he could still say, "As for God, His way is perfect; the word of the Lord is flawless" (2 Samuel 22:31).

2. The Bible's truths do not change, nor do they end.

One of the fundamental truths of the Bible is this: "The grass withers and the flowers fall but the word of our God stands forever" (Isaiah 40:8). Again, it is written: "Your word, O Lord, is eternal and stands firm in the heavens" (Psalms 119:89).

The counsel that was so powerful in the lives of the patriarchs and prophets can transform us, as well. God's truth doesn't change from generation to generation.

3. The solutions to life's deepest problems are in the Bible.

During the past thirty to thirty-five years, some have tried to convince the Christian community that people with "deep and disturbing" problems need psychiatric therapy, not biblical counsel. But the Bible is either God's sufficient Word or it isn't.

I can confidently say you and I will never face a problem in this life for which the Bible doesn't ultimately present a solution, either directly or indirectly. The Scriptures provide solid answers to life's most complex questions.

No wonder the psalmist says: "Your word is a lamp to my feet and a light for my path" (Psalm 119:105). Furthermore, "The unfolding of your words gives light" (Psalm 119:130).

God's Word is adequate and sufficient because it is forever right, and provides insight we cannot receive anywhere else under the sun. "Your statutes are forever right, give me understanding that I may live" (Psalm 119:144).

Can we trust the counsel of the Bible? Yes!

The law of the Lord is perfect, reviving the soul. The statutes of the Lord are trustworthy, making wise the simple. The precepts of the Lord are right, giving joy to the heart. The commands of the Lord are radiant, giving light to the eyes (Psalm 19:7-8).

When you read the Bible from cover to cover, you discover that it is a book of real people, with real problems, all needing real answers.

NOAH had a drinking problem.
ADAM had a blame-shifting problem.
CAIN was given to violence and murder.
AMNON committed rape and incest.
DAVID struggled with sexual lust.
HAMAN was a deceitful manipulator.
JEZEBEL was just plain mean.
MOSES had a temper problem.
ABRAHAM had a lying problem.
KING SAUL was consumed with jealousy.
SARAH suffered from pessimism and laughed at God.

THOMAS suffered from bouts with doubt.

PETER was impetuous, loud, and often spoke rashly.

BARAK could rightly be called timid and cowardly.

NADAB AND ABIHU had an attitude problem when it came to following God's instructions.

GEHAZI struggled with an honesty problem.

SIMON in Acts had an obvious greed problem.

Some of these people found the solution to their problems in God's spoken or written Word. Others blatantly disregarded God's Word to their own peril. Today the choice is ours. Will *we* take God at His Word, or not?

I began biblically counseling people thirty-nine years ago. The church where I've served as senior pastor for the past twenty-five years began its Biblical Lay Counseling Program in 1981. Since then, some four hundred men and women have received in-depth training and become certified Biblical Lay Counselors.

Currently, forty-five of these Biblical Lay Counselors are using God's Word to minister to scores of people in our church each month. While the counseling is offered free of charge, many counselees make contributions to the ministry so that still others can become trained Biblical Lay Counselors.

The results? Addictions are broken, marriages are healed, depression is shattered, disputes are settled, and hope is imparted to hundreds of men, women, and youth each year. The remedy in each case comes from God's Word, from looking at verse after verse that applies to the situation at hand.

Our church's Biblical Lay Counseling ministry has been built and thrives on the premise that there is no problem in a person's life for which there isn't a corresponding answer in God's Word. While this book doesn't cover every possible issue, it does address thirty-one of the most common problems for which people come to us, desperately seeking answers—real answers, answers that work, answers firmly based on God's life-changing Word!

The publishers and I are convinced you will always be greatly helped by going *first* to God's Word for the answer to the problem you're facing today—whatever it is—before going to anyone else for counsel. If the problem is complex or potentially life-threatening, then by all means, immediately seek out the counsel of those trained in using God's Word to help others. The section at the back of the book entitled "How to Find a Christian Counselor," will help you with this.

As I've written this book, I've prayed that God will use it to encourage and strengthen you—and in turn equip you to help counsel others from His Word. Since you'll likely find occasion to share this book with others, be sure to take a minute right now to write your name on the inside front cover. Then, always politely ask for it back!

You'll want to refer to this book again and again in the weeks and months and years ahead. Not that it has all the answers. But it does consistently point one and all to the Source of ultimate answers to life's thorniest problems.

God doesn't intend for us to live a life free of trouble, but He does want us to be whole and healthy, victorious over the problems we face. To that end I dedicate this book.

Abortion

In him [Jesus Christ] we have redemption through his blood,
the forgiveness of sins,
in accordance with the riches of God's grace.

EPHESIANS 1:7

■ ■ ■ ■ ■

Judy seemed to be the epitome of a godly Christian woman. Happily married and the mother of two small children, she was very gifted as a singer, organizer, and crusader for righteous causes.

But over the course of a few months, Judy dropped out of most of her church responsibilities, let her personal appearance begin to deteriorate, and began withdrawing from her husband. She became short-tempered with her children and often would go through bouts of deep depression.

Judy's husband initiated their counseling visit. After about an hour of delicate probing, the truth came out. Judy confessed she'd had an abortion when she was eighteen years old.

Judy's secret had been kept hushed for more than a decade, buried deep in the inner recesses of her and her parents' minds. No one else knew, except two or three unnamed staff members at the clinic where the abortion was performed. But gradually Judy's guilt pounded inside her until she could ignore it no longer.

With Judy's confession came God's forgiveness, cleansing, and healing. Her guilt resolved, Judy renewed her love for and commitment to the Lord, her husband, her children, and her church family.

No one can honestly deny the devastation caused by abortion on demand. It is a serious thing to choose to take another human life, especially when that person is your own flesh and blood.

True, some argue that a fetus isn't a person until birth occurs. However, Scripture suggests just the opposite—that life begins at conception. The biblical account of Jesus' conception, period of gestation, and birth certainly give credence to that: "You will be with child and give birth to a son, and you are to give him the name Jesus" (Luke 1:31).

Add to that the statement made about Elizabeth in the same chapter: "When Elizabeth heard Mary's greeting, the baby leaped in her womb" (Luke 1:41). Notice that it doesn't say, "the *fetus* leaped in her womb," or "a *blob of tissue* leaped in her womb." It says, "the *baby* leaped" for joy.

Some forty times Scripture refers to conception as the genesis of life in the womb of the mother.

> For you created my inmost being; you knit me together in my mother's womb. I praise you because I am fearfully and wonderfully made; your works are wonderful, I know that full well. My frame was not hidden from you when I was made in the secret place. When I was woven together in the depths of the earth, your eyes saw my unformed *body* (Psalm 139:13-16a, emphasis added).

Probably the most conclusive Scripture on this subject comes in God's remarks to Jeremiah, the prophet: "Before I formed you in the womb, I knew *you*. Before you were born, I set you apart" (Jeremiah 1:5, emphasis added).

The Lord unequivocally states that Jeremiah was Jeremiah long before birth. God knew exactly who he would be from the start. He was a *person* long before God finished fashioning his body.

How can anyone read such verses and not believe that life begins at conception? Thus, to abort a baby on demand is to take a life. From the first few pages of Genesis on, Scripture teaches that life is precious to God. The Lord commands us to respect its sanctity. Indeed, "Sons are a heritage from the Lord, children a reward from him" (Psalm 127:3).

If you have read this far, you may be saying, "I know, I know...abortion is murder, abortion is sin. My heart grieves within me over the evil I've done. But does this mean I'm condemned the rest of my life because I had an abortion or was a party to someone else's abortion?"

In His abundant grace, God says, "No, my child. Not only does My grace and mercy cover your sin, but I also want to give you My strength to get on with your life. Today I want to liberate you from the guilt Satan is using against you."

COUNSEL FROM GOD'S WORD

1. Understand that God isn't 'picky' with His pardon.

Nowhere in Scripture does it say God has a sin manual at His finger tips, which classifies some sins as wicked and others as terrible, horrible, or just plain bad. No, sin is sin in the eyes of God. But His grace covers a multitude of transgressions. While the *consequences* may vary from sin to sin, the *guilt* that comes from, say, coveting, doesn't differ from the guilt of lying, stealing, or unrighteous anger.

God's promise makes no distinction when He says:

Though your sins are like scarlet, they shall be as white as snow;
though they are red as crimson, they shall be like wool (Isaiah
1:18b).

2. Understand the true nature of a loving God.

While God has established the standard by which He intends us to live, He also is loving and patient. In giving thanks for the boundless depths of God's love, the psalmist says: "For great is your love, reaching to the heavens; your faithfulness reaches to the skies" (Psalm 57:10).

The psalmist also reminds us:

The Lord is compassionate and gracious, slow to anger, abounding
in love. He will not always accuse, nor will he harbor his anger forever; he does not treat us as our sins deserve or repay us according

to our iniquities. For as high as the heavens are above the earth, so great is his love for those who fear him (Psalm 103:8-11).

In our depravity, as members of a fallen race, you and I are capable of heinous crimes and sin. But no matter how low we stoop, how horribly we sin, our sin will never be greater than God's grace.

The apostle Paul put it this way: "But where sin increased, grace increased all the more" (Romans 5:20). That promise isn't intended to be a "license" for us to go out and see how much we can sin, so God can use His endless supply of grace. It is intended to reassure you and me that when we fail, do something foolish, or fall into the worst sin we can think of, there is an inexhaustible supply of divine grace to cover our sin.

3. Remember, God has forgotten your past sins and He wants you to forget them, too.

We used to sing a chorus years ago that went like this:

Gone, gone, gone, gone, all my sins are gone,
Now my soul is free and in my heart's a song.
Buried in the deepest sea,
yes, that's good enough for me.
I shall live eternally, praise God—
my sins are gone!

The prophet, addressing God, makes this great affirmation:

You will again have compassion on us; you will tread our sins underfoot and hurl all our iniquities into the depths of the sea (Micah 7:19).

What a promise! You can lay hold of it and believe it! God has removed our guilt and no longer sees our many sins. The psalmist says, "As far as the east is from the west, so far has he removed our transgressions from us" (Psalm 103:12).

Paul put it into good perspective: "Forgetting what is behind and straining toward what is ahead, I press on" (Philippians 3:13b-14a).

If God says you're forgiven, and He has agreed never to bring up that sin again, then believe him—you are forgiven! If He won't bring up the sin, why should we? To do so is to doubt His Word.

God would have you now minister to others anguishing over the same guilt you once experienced. Because of what the Lord has done in your life, you're in a unique position. Study God's Word further and make yourself available to help others.

■ ■ ■ ■ ■

More biblical counsel

I JOHN 1:7-9

PSALM 103:3-4

PSALM 42:11

ISAIAH 40:31

DEUTERONOMY 33:27

PSALM 51

PSALM 32

Adultery

But among you there must not be even a hint of sexual immorality,
or of any kind of impurity, or of greed,
because these are improper for God's holy people.

EPHESIANS 5:3

■ ■ ■ ■ ■

The pain is indescribable! You and I can't even begin to calculate it. I'm talking about the pain that comes to a spouse when he or she discovers that his or her spouse has violated something very precious and sacred—the sexual bond that exists in marriage.

A man whom I had lunch with recently, said, "I will spend a lifetime paying for a few short minutes of physical pleasure." He was referring to an affair that resulted in sexual unfaithfulness.

When the Bible talks about the "one-flesh" relationship, it's signifying that, in marriage, a couple agrees to experience sexual closeness and intimacy only with each other. That physical oneness is part of the marriage bond and covenant.

The apostle Paul substantiates the sacredness of that oneness by asking:

Do you not know that your bodies are members of Christ himself?
Shall I then take the members of Christ and unite them with a
prostitute? Never! Do you not know that he who unites himself
with a prostitute is one with her body? (1 Corinthians 6:15-16).

The sex act in marriage makes two become one. To break that oneness by having sex with someone else is to break faith with both God and one's husband or wife.

Why do people commit adultery? Apart from selfishness, which is the root cause of every sin, there are several other reasons:

1. Lack of sexual satisfaction.

While this is not an excuse to seek sex elsewhere, it somewhat explains why some people—especially men—commit adultery. Unrealistic expectations are often at the heart of such dissatisfaction.

2. A person's own sinful, sexual desire.

The Bible says:

> But each one is tempted when, by his own evil desire, he is dragged away and enticed. Then, after desire has conceived, it gives birth to sin; and sin, when it is full-grown, gives birth to death (James 1:14-15).

3. Others are driven into adultery by a demanding, scolding, or critical spouse.

Some seek to take revenge against such a spouse by sleeping with someone else.

4. Loneliness and a sense that no one cares.

Some end up committing adultery in a desperate attempt to find intimacy with another human being.

5. Sexual addictions.

Sometimes adultery is committed by someone overtaken by sexual addiction. Such addictions often go back years, to one's youth.

If you have committed adultery, God's Word has some clear answers for you.

COUNSEL FROM GOD'S WORD

1. Understand from Scripture where adultery begins.

Adultery begins in our minds and hearts—as we think about sexual immorality and entertain lust for the opposite sex.

Jesus taught this when He said:

For out of the heart come evil thoughts, murder, adultery, sexual immorality, theft, false testimony, slander. These are what make a man unclean (Matthew 15:19-20a).

2. Agree with what the Lord says about adultery.

What does God think of adultery? Does He wink at it? Does He ever excuse it? The seventh commandment is clear: "You shall not commit adultery" (Exodus 20:14).

The Mosaic law also says:

If a man commits adultery with another man's wife—with the wife of his neighbor—both the adulterer and the adulteress must be put to death (Leviticus 20:10).

Elsewhere we read: "But a man who commits adultery lacks judgment; whoever does so destroys himself" (Proverbs 6:32).

God calls adultery a "horrible" thing:

And among the prophets of Jerusalem I have seen something horrible: They commit adultery and live a lie. They strengthen the hands of evildoers, so that no one turns from his wickedness. They are all like Sodom; the people of Jerusalem are like Gomorrah (Jeremiah 23:14).

3. Confess your sin to God and forsake it immediately.

It's important for us to let God know we're willing to call adultery the same thing He calls it—sin. True repentance compels us to abandon the sin, forsake it, and get away from everything that would remind us of it. The Bible says:

He who conceals his sins does not prosper, but whoever confesses and renounces them finds mercy (Proverbs 28:13).

4. Apologize and ask forgiveness from all whom you have offended.

Confessing sin to God is essential, but it's not enough. We must go back to the people we sinned against and ask their forgiveness. The Lord Himself instructs us:

> Therefore if you are offering your gift at the altar and there remem-
> ber that your brother has something against you, leave your gift
> there in front of the altar. First go and be reconciled to your brother,
> then come and offer your gift (Matthew 5:23-24).

I know it says if "your brother has something against you." But whether or not the other person has something against you, or you have something against him or her or in any way have offended that person, you still need to go and make it right.

Some would disagree with this advice, believing that we need to "let sleeping dogs lie." This is a very controversial issue. For instance, if you committed adultery against your spouse years ago, might it not be destructive to tell him or her now, after all these years? It could be. This is a judgment call a person has to make after earnestly praying for God's wisdom:

> If any of you lacks wisdom, he should ask God, who gives generously
> to all without finding fault, and it will be given to him (James 1:5).

5. Focus on God and His Word rather than your sin.

I know of no one who has committed adultery who just woke up one morning and decided to cheat on his or her spouse. Instead, it was in the "think tank" long before it ever became a physical reality. Jesus sternly warns us against adulterous thoughts:

> You have heard that it was said, "Do not commit adultery." But I tell
> you that anyone who looks at a woman lustfully has already com-
> mitted adultery with her in his heart (Matthew 5:27).

Someone has said:

Sow a thought, reap an act. Sow an act, reap a habit. Sow a habit, reap your character. Sow your character, and reap your destiny.

That is well said, and true! I suggest you write it in the flyleaf of your Bible or notebook.

If you want to never fall into the trap of adultery again, it will require that you "have the mind of Christ." But one doesn't suddenly *get* the mind of Christ. It comes by focusing and meditating on His Word.

Since, then, you have been raised with Christ, set your hearts on things above, where Christ is seated at the right hand of God. Set your minds on things above, not on earthly things (Colossians 3:1-2).

There is only one way to set your mind on things above. Get into God's Word daily, and allow that Word to shape and mold and direct your thinking.

6. Bask in God's forgiveness!

We are told in Scripture that Jesus' blood covers *all* our sins—past, present, and daily (1 John 1:7). If you have fallen into sexual sin, Christ's blood avails for even that. His cleansing and forgiveness are waiting to pour into your life, like water waits to pour out of a faucet.

The apostle John reminds us:

If we confess our sins, he is faithful and just, and will forgive us our sins and purify us from all unrighteousness (1 John 1:9).

If you're not sure how to pray to God and ask for His forgiveness, please use this prayer:

Dear God, I have sinned, violating your law and the purity You gave me in Christ. I confess my sin of adultery to You and ask Your forgiveness for it. Cleanse me, Lord, of all impurity, and enable me to appropriate the power You have made available for me to go and sin no more. Amen.

■ ■ ■ ■ ■

More biblical counsel

HEBREWS 13:4

JOHN 8:11

ISAIAH 1:16-18

I CORINTHIANS 6:15-20

LUKE 15:11-14

JAMES 5:14-15

GALATIANS 2:20

I JOHN 2:1-2

Abusive
Behavior

Make sure that nobody pays back wrong for wrong,
but always try to be kind to each other and to everyone else.

1 THESSALONIANS 5:15

∎ ∎ ∎ ∎ ∎

T he word "abuse" may be overused today, but it's the only word that
describes the kind of behavior some people use to inflict pain and suffering on others.

Tina and John had a beautiful wedding attended by many family members and friends. Both had been raised in Christian homes and brought up to
cherish biblical values. At the marriage altar, they promised to love, cherish,
and protect one another. As they drove off after the wedding reception, one
attendee was heard to say, "If ever there was an ideal couple, they're it!"

Only three months into the marriage, however, we learned from a teary-
eyed Tina that things weren't going well at all. Whenever John let his anger get
out of control, he verbally abused Tina. She was so hurt by his insults, threats,
and foul language that she was ready to leave John and forget their marriage
had ever taken place. Such abuse revealed a side of John she had never seen
before their wedding.

John would always apologize to Tina, begging for her forgiveness and promising he would never do it again. But within days, the loud and abusive yelling would start all over. Tina had never heard her father swear, let alone verbally abuse her mother in such cruel ways. This compounded her shock and dismay. She began to wonder if John's fits of rage would soon turn into physical abuse. She became so fearful of John that she even had difficulty sleeping at night.

John followed a pattern that abusive people almost always follow:

- Harsh blaming of others
- Verbal accusations
- Verbal intimidation
- Verbal abuse

The only thing John had not done was become physically violent, but that was next.

Verbal abuse often is only the beginning. It may precede physical abuse, sexual abuse, child abuse, and abuse of the elderly, the sick, and the handicapped.

Behind all abuse is a temperament pattern brought on by sin and disobedience. The abusive person usually possesses the following traits.

I. The need to feel important.

One universal trait among abusers is a deep-seated desire to be elevated to a position of importance and significance. Abusers always look for someone to belittle, whether a spouse, child, neighbor, or co-worker. Many display an obvious absence of humility.

This attitude of superiority is in direct conflict with God's standard and God's Word. Scripture commands us, "Do nothing out of selfish ambition or vain conceit, but in humility consider others better than yourselves" (Philippians 2:3).

The apostle Paul also exposes and condemns this attitude in his letter to the Roman church:

> For by the grace given me I say to every one of you: Do not think
> of yourself more highly than you ought, but rather think of yourself

with sober judgment, in accordance with the measure of faith God has given you (Romans 12:3).

2. The compulsion to be a controller.

Another universal trait among abusers is an inner compulsion to control. When such control can't be obtained in peaceful ways, abusers resort to loud shouting, name-calling, and threats. They may seek to control the other person's schedule, activities, thoughts, decisions, or feelings.

The compulsion to control only affirms a severe lack of respect, coupled with a distrust in God. The Bible makes it clear that our relationships to other people should be based on respect and honor: "Be devoted to one another in brotherly love. Honor one another above yourselves" (Romans 12:10).

Paul goes on to say in that same chapter: "If it is possible, as far as it depends on you, live at peace with everyone" (Romans 12:18).

While children need structure and limits, they also need to know they're trusted by their parents. The same goes for husbands and wives.

While the biblical role of the wife is to be in submission to her husband, the husband needs to demonstrate a great deal of trust in his wife. A husband's attempts to control his wife not only reveal he distrusts her, they also confirm he is insecure. His efforts to demand an inordinate degree of loyalty from his wife are only futile attempts to gain a sense of security.

3. Many abusers are abuse victims themselves.

What people inflict on others is often a carryover from what they themselves suffered earlier in life. That doesn't excuse the abuse or the abuser, but it often helps explain his or her behavior. This is especially true of men who physically and verbally abuse members of their own families.

4. Abusers often have a high degree of stress in their lives.

They are usually people who are extremely frustrated over their jobs, their weight, their health, their physical appearance, or their general lot in life. Not only is their temper extremely short, they also seem unable or unwilling to cope with even the slightest disturbance or detour in their lives.

I've heard psychologists and professional therapists say that it takes months, even years for an abuser to change his or her conduct. I believe this demonstrates a lack of faith in God's power and a denial of the effectiveness of His Word.

COUNSEL FROM GOD'S WORD

1. Stop shifting the blame for your abusive behavior.

Any explanation given for people's abusive behavior can become an excuse or justification for such behavior. Abusiveness is sinful behavior, the epitome of disobedience to God's Word and God's standard for life.

Much of the time abusers blame their behavior on the very people they abuse, claiming they were "egging on" the abuser or "asking for it." Other abusers blame their parents, their home conditions, poverty, genetics, or a combination of all of the above.

When the prodigal son came home, he said, "I have sinned" (Luke 15:21). He didn't say, "I acted foolishly because it was in my genes." Instead, he accepted full responsibility for his actions.

When King David repented over his adultery with Bathsheba, he said, "Against you [Lord], you only, have I sinned, and done what is evil in your sight." He didn't say, "She was asking for it" by taking a bath where David could see her from the roof of his house.

2. Allow God to apply judgment and penalty to others.

Many abusers excuse their behavior by saying, "Someone has to uphold the standard around here and punish the guilty."

But it is not our responsibility to mete out punishment or play the role of someone else's conscience. God will apply due punishment on the right people at the right time for the right reason—and He certainly won't hold the abuser guiltless.

Do not take revenge my friends, but leave room for God's wrath, for
it is written, "It is mine to avenge; I will repay, says the Lord"
(Romans 12:19).

The "get even" department is headed up by God alone. It's never our responsibility to even the score.

3. Remember, it is a sign of weakness—not strength—to be abusive.

Anyone can bully and intimidate, but it takes a real man or a real woman to be humble in front of others. Whenever an abusive person explodes and takes his anger out on his victims, he isn't solving anything; he's only creating worse problems. James 1:20 says, "for man's anger does not bring about the righteous life that God desires."

4. Admit that your abusive behavior dishonors God.

Every time abusive behavior is displayed, glory is taken away from God. Scripture says, "So, whether you eat or drink or *whatever* you do, do it all for the glory of God" (1 Corinthians 10:31, emphasis added).

5. Ask forgiveness from those you have abused.

If you want to be truly free from the bondage of abusive behavior, part of repentance demands that you go and ask for the forgiveness of those whom you have abused. God won't change your life until you are willing to seek forgiveness from those you've mistreated.

6. Ask for and claim God's forgiveness.

No one really understands the power of words. Words can bruise, sting, slice, and harm people for years to come. If you have been abusive in speech to your father or mother, spouse, child, or someone else, get to your knees and ask God to forgive you. He will! Thank Him for His forgiveness, then rise to your feet determined to never again use that kind of speech or force in your life.

Fortunately, John did just that. But the healing process began only once he got on his knees in humility and sincere repentance. He was discipled by an older Christian man for more than six months. They focused on those passages of Scripture that deal with ego, pride, control, and our attitude toward others. John made a one-hundred-eighty-degree turn during that period and learned that he didn't have to continue in an abusive pattern just because he came from a verbally abusive home.

John allowed the Lord to break the yoke of abuse that had been passed down from generation to generation. Today, he and Tina have a great marriage and are providing a loving, nurturing Christian home for their two little ones.

If you have abused someone else, immediately make yourself accountable to a mature Christian leader in your church, someone of the same sex, and be willing to stand corrected when he or she senses you are returning to your old ways again.

Make this prayer yours:

Lord, I'm truly sorry for my controlling and demeaning behavior toward _____ (mention individuals by name). I've hurt them so deeply. Please forgive me. I repent of my past behavior. I surrender all of that to You right now. From this moment on, I ask you to bring conviction even to my thoughts when I'm feeling out of control and potentially abusive.

■ ■ ■ ■ ■

More biblical counsel

EPHESIANS 5:25-29

EPHESIANS 6:4

I CORINTHIANS 6:9-11

I PETER 3:7

PROVERBS 3:34

PROVERBS 8:13

PROVERBS 11:2

PROVERBS 12:9

PROVERBS 13:10

PROVERBS 15:25

PROVERBS 16:2-5

I CORINTHIANS 10:32

PHILIPPIANS 2:1-6

JAMES 4:6-7

Adversity

Though the fig tree does not bud and there are no grapes on the vines,
though the olive crop fails and the fields produce no food,
though there are no sheep in the pen and no cattle in the stalls,
Yet I will rejoice in the Lord, I will be joyful in God my Savior.
HABAKKUK 3:17-18

·····

"I just can't understand...Why is all this happening to me?"

"I feel so overwhelmed. What have I done to deserve this?"

"If God is fair and just, why doesn't He put a stop to all this suffering? Why does He let such horrible things happen to such innocent people?"

"Why did God let my child die? Why? *Why?* I thought He was a God of love. Doesn't He know what's just happened? Doesn't He care?"

You've heard such questions...maybe you've even asked them yourself.

I'll call him Billy. His life nose-dived when he was only two years old. His father died, and his mother—feeling overwhelmed because she had no money or means of support with which to raise her twin boys—abandoned her two sons. Billy and his brother were raised by grandparents. Then at age twelve, Billy was diagnosed with stomach cancer.

I made weekly visits when Billy's condition got really bad. Just before he turned fourteen, Billy began suffering the kind of pain morphine can't even begin to touch. The last week of his life was worse than being condemned to a torture chamber. After crying out in pain for days, his hoarse voice was merci-fully silenced by death.

When Billy died, his grandfather became very angry and shouted, "Why didn't Billy even get a crack at life?"

In such moments of agonizing misery, there is no such thing as a neatly written list of reasons why, only submission to the sovereignty of God.

Our own experiences confirm what Eliphaz said to Job: "Yet man is born to trouble as surely as sparks fly upward" (Job 5:7). Solomon later stated: "A poor man's field may produce abundant food but injustice sweeps it away" (Proverbs 13:23). And, "A friend loves at all times, and a brother is born for adversity" (Proverbs 17:17).

In our kitchen, my wife and I have a rather famous brand of salt. The container features the picture of a girl walking with an umbrella over her head. Next to the picture is the statement, "When it rains...it pours!" The idea behind this is, "When it's raining outside, our brand of salt still pours out of the box!" But we all know that little saying has another meaning: "When trouble comes, it comes all at once." If you're not old enough to know that statement is true, hang on!

Adversity comes in many styles and colors, and is no respecter of persons:
- Unemployment
- Diabetes
- Arthritic pain
- Migraine headaches
- Crushed vertebrae
- Brain tumor
- Cystic fibrosis
- Mental handicaps
- Alzheimer's
- Paralysis
- Broken engagement
- Unwanted divorce
- SIDS
- AIDS

- Bankruptcy
- Parkinson's Disease
- Multiple sclerosis
- Victim of marital infidelity
- Loss of eyesight or hearing
- Death of a parent, spouse, or child
- Single parenthood
- Amputation of a limb

There really aren't enough pages in this book to list every type of adversity, are there?

Job wrote the manual on adversity. God blessed him with ten children but they all died in one fell swoop, while having dinner together. Job owned eleven thousand head of livestock but lost them all that same day. He employed a large number of servants but virtually all were killed in a single attack. Soon thereafter, Job's entire body was covered with horrible sores. His own wife turned on him, urging him to curse God, give up, and die. Put all that together and you have someone who became an instant authority on the painful, devastating subject of adversity.

Overnight Job lost his health, wealth, and family— everything! Yet Job didn't shake an angry fist at God and cry out, "Why, Lord?" Instead, his response was: "The Lord gave and the Lord has taken away; may the name of the Lord be praised" (Job 1:21b).

Although Job's suffering was public, we sometimes attempt to hide our own times of adversity from our peers. Solomon wrote, "Even in laughter the heart may ache, and joy may end in grief" (Proverbs 14:13). While we may try to conceal our adversity from others, however, it has a way of "bleeding through."

The answer to adversity isn't toughing it out, in our own strength.

COUNSEL FROM GOD'S WORD

When you feel buffeted by adversity, God's Word can become your strong tower, if you allow it to. It has far more to say about our response to adversity than we have room to print in this chapter. However, here are some broad principles from Scripture which show how to respond properly in times of trouble.

1. Recognize that adversity may be the result of our wrong choices.

A young college-age man recently said to me, "I got a $65 speeding ticket. What is God trying to say to me?"

Simple: "You were speeding."

Solomon wisely said, "The way of the unfaithful is hard" (Proverbs 13:15). We may live in a free country, but there is no such thing as a moral-free universe. We all have to live with the consequences of our actions.

King David learned this the hard way, didn't he? What was the result of his adulterous fling with Bathsheba? Guilt, murder, cover-up, exposure, the tragic death of his newborn son, and heartache the rest of his life. It's ridiculous to sow sin and then expect to reap God's pleasure, blessing, and reward.

2. Realize adversity can be the chisel God uses to shape us up.

God sometimes allows or brings adversity into our lives to test the "stuff" of which we're made and prepare us for even greater tests ahead. His goal is to strengthen the fiber of our faith in Him.

The apostle Peter says trials come into our lives "so that your faith, of greater worth than gold, which perishes, even though refined by fire, may be proved genuine" (1 Peter 1:6-7).

How true!

If you're going through the "furnace" of adversity right now, read Peter's words once again. God is using that fire to consume the base metals in your life so you can be stronger. The sun melts chocolate, but hardens clay. What it does depends on the consistency of the object upon which it shines.

How you respond in times of adversity depends on what you're made of. Listen to what James says:

> When all kinds of trial and temptations crowd into your lives, my brothers, don't resent them as intruders, but welcome them as friends. Realize that they come to test your faith, and produce in you the quality of endurance. But let the process go on until that endurance is fully developed, and you will find that you have become men of mature character (James 1:2-4, Phillips).

Go back and read Job, chapter 23. In acknowledging God's sovereignty, Job said, "He knows the way I take, when he has tested me I will come forth as gold" (Job 23:10).

3. Remember adversity comes so God may be glorified in and through our lives.

Hard times glorify God, either now or ultimately. The apostle Paul was well acquainted with affliction, yet he could say, "our light and momentary troubles are achieving for us an eternal glory that far outweighs them all" (2 Corinthians 4:17).

Powerful words!

The "glory" adversity produces isn't ours, it's God's. He is glorified in and through our adversity because it gives Him the opportunity to show Himself strong, faithful, and redeeming. As we see those attributes manifested, we cannot help but glorify the Lord.

4. Understand how adversity can be God's way to prompt us to rely on Him.

Ever since we were toddlers, each of us has had a tendency to want to "do it myself." But sometimes we need to be tossed flat on our backs in order to look up and get a new perspective. In his letter to the Corinthians, Paul confided that he had suffered horrible adversity in the Roman province of Asia:

> Indeed in our hearts we felt the sentence of death. But this happened that we might not rely on ourselves, but on God who raises the dead (2 Corinthians 1:9).

While trying to escape the wrath and terror of King Saul, the psalmist David wrote these words:

> No king is saved by the size of his army, no warrior escapes by his great strength. A horse is a vain hope for deliverance; despite all its great strength, it cannot save. But the eyes of the Lord are on those who fear him, on those whose hope is in his unfailing love (Psalm 33:16-18a).

Is God loving and fair when He allows the storms of life to whip all about us? Scripture assures us, yes. "Will not the judge of all the earth do right?" (Genesis 18:25b).

That doesn't mean all our questions will be answered in this life. But Billy's grandfather came to understand that the Lord who "gives and takes away" is in sovereign control of all that happens to us. And Billy's surviving twin brother went on to become a physician, dedicating his life to others' health.

If you're going through adversity right now, rely on God. Put your hope and your desire for respite in Him and Him alone.

■ ■ ■ ■ ■

More biblical counsel

JOB 8:3

PSALM 18

PSALM 23

PSALM 27:1-2

PSALM 37

PSALM 40:1-8

PSALM 46:1

PSALM 55:22

PSALM 56:3-4

PSALM 62:1-2

PSALM 69

PSALM 73

PSALM 145:14

ISAIAH 26:3

ISAIAH 30:15

2 CORINTHIANS 1:3-4

MATTHEW 11:28-29

Affair Victims

Above all, love each other deeply,
because love covers over a multitude of sins.

I PETER 4:8

■ ■ ■ ■ ■

I 'll call her Beth to conceal her identity, but her story is true to the word
Shortly before midnight, she phoned me, screaming hysterically, "I'm
ruined, I'm ruined! It's all over; my marriage is over!

"Pastor, Sam has had an affair! He's cheated on me. You've got to come
over right now or I'm walking out of this house and never coming back again!"

Twenty minutes later, while two small children slept in their bedroom, I
arrived to find this couple sitting in their living room—their marriage hanging
together by a thread.

By now Beth's violent anger had subsided. She was all tears, convulsively
crying her heart out in her devastation. Sam was scared to death, at a loss for
words.

It turned out Sam's assistant at work was a recent divorcee. The mother
of a three-year-old, she confided in Sam, seeking solace, direction, and sympa-
thy. An emotional bond developed, and soon they were having coffee together.
That led to dinner together, later to heavy petting, then finally to sex at her
apartment.

The affair had been going on for about two months. Beth knew something was wrong during that time because Sam would hardly touch her. It

might have gone on even longer except Beth finally called over to the woman's apartment and, saying there was an emergency, asked if Sam was there. Thinking one of the children was ill, Sam came to the phone—and was caught! Once home, Sam owned up to the whole thing and begged Beth's forgiveness.

What happens when you discover the one you love—and the one you thought loved you—is having an affair with someone else? First, it's important to understand the underlying reasons for such a betrayal of one's marriage vows.

WHAT CAUSES AFFAIRS?

You may say, "That's simple. It's deliberate disobedience to God's Word that prompts a married partner to commit sexual immorality." But what causes such disobedience?

1. Allowing relationships at work to get too personal.

Many spend forty hours a week at the office, some longer. Most work with people of the opposite sex and often are thrown into close proximity with them.

If someone allows himself to become emotionally dependent on another person of the opposite sex, eventually sexual desires are aroused, even if the person has the most wonderful spouse in the whole world.

At work, Sam was thrown into very close physical proximity with his assistant since they had to sit for hours and go over electrical bids together. A hand on the shoulder, a friendly slap on the knee, and a spirit of teamwork all drew them closer and closer together.

In addition, both were required to work overtime. It was just the two of them in the office until eight or nine some evenings. With no one else there, no one watching...the temptation eventually became too great.

Couple that with the fact that Sam's assistant was lonely, emotionally down, and starving for the security of a close relationship, and you have a gasoline and match situation ready to explode.

2. Unmet needs at home.

Affairs often develop when one spouse isn't getting his or her needs met at home. Both husband and wife have sexual needs, but the wife also needs companionship. She longs to be wanted, loved, romanced, cared for, fussed over, and communicated with. When that need isn't met at home, there's always a guy somewhere waiting to fill it.

A man's primary need is sexual gratification with his wife. When night after night he's postponed, put off, or reluctantly given in to, he becomes very open to other women who are putting out the signals.

Lack of sex at home doesn't give anyone a license to have sex outside of marriage, but it does sometimes explain why a man enters into an illicit relationship, thinking of his own needs, not those of his wife.

As it turned out, Beth was volunteering at both church and a local preschool. On top of that, she was redecorating part of their house. When evenings came, she basically collapsed in a deep sleep. Sam's needs were put off time after time—not on purpose, but through lack of discernment.

Not only was Sam a panacea for his assistant at work who didn't have a husband, she in turn showed him some of the attention Beth wasn't showing at home. Unless such a cycle is deliberately broken, immediately, an affair is in the making.

3. Overextended schedules.

Couples often have a way of overextending themselves to the point of neglecting each other. It's not a planned thing; it usually happens almost by accident. I knew one couple who were committed either individually or as a couple five out of every seven nights a week. Most of their days were full, too. By the time they did find a free night together, they often were too tired to enjoy much intimacy.

4. Both spouses working outside the home.

When a wife decides to work outside the home, her relationship with her husband changes. First of all, she usually has a male supervisor who, in a sense, shares headship with her husband. Second, if she's not careful, she may begin to feel independent from her husband while in the work place. It's not surprising that more than eighty percent of all affairs begin at work.

5. The "look what I missed" syndrome.

When tiresome routine enters a marriage, it can be lethal. Several years after a young man and woman marry, one or both may begin to muse, "Hmmm, I wonder if I've missed anything?" This is especially true if the road has been bumpy along the way, finances have been a problem, and two or more children have come along.

Sometimes this syndrome doesn't hit until couples reach their forties or early fifties. An almost demonic desire can emerge. Suddenly one spouse decides, "I've been faithful all these years and, frankly, I'm bored. It's about time to develop some new 'interests.' " This often is true if several peers or colleagues already are doing the same thing.

After having an affair and later repenting, one man confided, "I left my wife and kids to move in with what I thought was the most exciting woman in the world. I wasn't there a week before I realized that what I left was so much better than what I had found."

That's often how affairs end. The show window may be attractive, but the warehouse is empty.

6. Spouses allow their relationship with God to grow cold.

This, of course, is the basic reason all affairs get started. I've never counseled anyone who's had an affair who had not first drifted away from prayer and Bible reading, and eventually Christian service and even church attendance.

Nearly everyone will be tempted at one time or another to have an affair. It's almost a given! The only sure defense is cultivating a healthy and vibrant spiritual life, so you'll be strong enough to fight off the temptation.

THE GAMUT OF YOUR FEELINGS

If you've been cheated on, you'll probably go through a range of feelings.

1. Anger

This is usually someone's first emotion, after the initial shock. The rage is rarely focused, however, all on one person. Your anger may be directed first at your spouse, then at the other person, then at yourself. "How did I let this happen?" Anger is a natural reaction to betrayal. "I've been had, I've had the wool pulled over my eyes, I've been deceived."

2. Hurt

Anger usually gives way to hurt. Had you received the news your spouse had died it would not hurt nearly as badly as this news. It's the hurt of rejection, and there's no hurt deeper. It's the hurt that your spouse actually found someone he or she is more interested in than you. It's hurt for the kids, if you have any. It's hurt over what your parents will think of you and of your spouse. It's the hurt of trust broken. Of all the feelings, this is probably the most profound and lasts the longest.

3. Despair

Nothing brings on despair faster than learning your marriage has been violated. One woman wrote to me after learning her husband was unfaithful: "All my life has been wrapped up in my Lord and my husband. Now only my Lord remains faithful." You could read the depths of despair between the lines of her letter. Feelings of depression and emptiness and hopelessness are often very real for affair victims.

4. Fear

From anger to hurt to despair, we now come to fear. Affair victims experience many kinds of fear. If you are a woman and your husband has had an affair, and is unwilling to break it off, you fear not only the loss of your mate and the father of your children, but also the provider of your material needs. How will you live? Where will you live? How will you support your children?

If you are a man whose wife has had the affair, other fears loom. If a divorce or separation occurs, what about the kids? What about living arrangements? What about the stigma? Will it happen again? If you forgive her and the two of you stay together, will things ever be like they once were?

5. Frustration and confusion

Feelings of total confusion often prevail at a time like this. You may even feel like giving up. On top of this, feelings of inadequacy, worthlessness, and uselessness may abound. What do you do?

COUNSEL FROM GOD'S WORD

The Bible, God's Word, is your source of greatest hope at a time like this. Every word is true to life. You'll discover it will not only comfort you, but also instruct you on what your appropriate response should be.

1. Remember the love you vowed to your spouse.

During your wedding ceremony, you promised to "love and cherish" your spouse. Biblically, such *agape* love is to be unconditional, whatever happens: "it keeps no record of wrongs" (1 Corinthians 13:5).

Jesus urges us to love one another the same way He loves us. Even though His disciples denied and betrayed Him, Jesus loved them to the end. After His resurrection, He deliberately reaffirmed His love and forgiveness. That's unconditional love!

In the same way, reassure your spouse that you love him or her, even though you are terribly brokenhearted. Any hope of a healed marriage depends largely on your love staying constant.

2. Decide now to forgive your spouse.

Scripture gives us many reasons to forgive, but perhaps the most important one is found in Ephesians 4. You need to forgive your spouse because God has forgiven you! Forgiveness doesn't condone the action of the offender, it simply releases the offender from having to try to pay for that offense.

Second, you need to forgive your spouse in order to prevent Satan from taking advantage of you. "Do not let the sun go down while you are still angry, and do not give the devil a foothold" (Ephesians 4:26-27). Hebrews 12:15 also warns against allowing a root of bitterness to grow within us.

You may be saying, "But adultery was the one sin for which Jesus gave us permission to get a divorce!" Yes, that's partially true. Jesus did say: "I tell you that anyone who divorces his wife, except for marital unfaithfulness, and marries another woman commits adultery" (Matthew 19:9).

But earlier, Jesus said Moses allowed divorce only because of the hardness of men's hearts. In other words, you're not "required" to get a divorce because your mate commits adultery, even though it is permitted. But never forget: *your responsibility to forgive your spouse always takes precedence over your right to divorce.* Every time a judge says, "Divorce granted," someone has failed to forgive his or her spouse.

3. Never hold what your spouse did over his or her head.

True forgiveness doesn't go back and dig up the matter repeatedly as a lever to get what you want. When it comes to forgiveness, there are five *nevers:*

- *Never* use what your spouse did in the past to bring him or her back into line.
- *Never* bring up the affair in conversation again. If your spouse wants to bring it up, fine, but otherwise, leave it in the past.
- *Never* attempt to "get even" by deciding you should have an affair yourself.
- *Never* snoop in your spouse's mail, calendar, personal belongings, dresser drawers, or closets. Such actions only confirm you still don't trust your spouse.
- *Never* fail to stand up for your mate when he or she is put down by others, especially by relatives.

Remember that "love covers a multitude of sins" (1 Peter 4:8).

4. Resolve to shore up your responsibilities to your spouse.

Although no affair can ever be justified, sometimes they come about partially because of the "innocent party's" failure to meet certain needs.

Ask yourself, "Have I been loving? Have I shown attention? Have I focused on meeting my spouse's needs? Have I had a good attitude even when we've differed? Have I tried to remain attractive for my spouse?"

A good Scripture to meditate on is this: "So, if you think you are standing firm, be careful that you don't fall" (1 Corinthians 10:12). Good advice! Before we place *all* the blame on our spouse, it may be good to do some personal investigation into our own lives.

5. Resolve to pray daily for your spouse.

If you weren't doing it before, resolve to do it now! Pray for your spouse. In Scripture, we're commanded to "pray for each other so that you may be healed" (James 5:16).

Pray specifically:

- that your spouse will be protected by God;
- that your spouse will accept forgiveness;
- that your spouse will have a healthy ongoing repentance;
- that your spouse would draw closer to the Lord;
- that your spouse will be able to minister to others sometime in the future because of what he or she has gone through.

6. Learn to laugh with your spouse again.

As they were reconciling, one couple asked me point blank, "Will we ever laugh again?" My answer was a resounding yes! But I told them they would have to work at it. The trauma of an affair has a way of robbing all the joy and laughter from a marriage. If you're the victim of the affair, make sure you take the initiative to bring joy and humor back into your relationship. The Bible says, "A cheerful heart is good medicine" (Proverbs 17:22).

7. Make sure you comfort and reassure your spouse.

This may seem hard, but more than once you will need to say, "I love you. It's in the past, let's get on with our lives. I've forgiven you." The goal isn't permanent discipline, but rather reconciliation.

Writing to the Corinthian church after they had disciplined someone, Paul urged them to now forgive and comfort the offender:

The punishment inflicted on him by the majority is sufficient for him. Now instead, you ought to forgive and comfort him, so that he will not be overwhelmed by excessive sorrow. I urge you, therefore, to reaffirm your love for him (2 Corinthians 2:6-8).

In other words, back off. As many times as it takes, keep telling your spouse that you love him or her. Comfort your spouse. No, this isn't condoning or making light of the sin. Instead, you're saying you really care and aren't about to let your spouse's failure create a permanent rift between the two of you.

Do these principles work?

Before I left Beth and Sam's home at about two that morning, she agreed not to file for divorce. Over the next few days the three of us went over many Scriptures together. About a week later, Beth threw her arms around Sam, forgave him, and agreed to work through the issues at hand. Although their relationship was far from perfect, and their many wounds had yet to heal, within a few weeks Beth and Sam were on their way toward putting the pieces of their marriage back together again.

How was Beth able to forgive Sam, continue to live with him, and—most importantly—trust him? Only by God's power and encouragement through His Word.

Beth and Sam did laugh again, and today have a happy home and family life. Remember, an affair doesn't need to mean the end of a marriage.

■ ■ ■ ■ ■

More biblical counsel

>PSALM 34:18
>
>JAMES 1:14-15
>
>PROVERBS 5:15-18
>
>PSALM 91:1
>
>PSALM 30:5
>
>PSALM 46:1-2
>
>PHILIPPIANS 4:6
>
>PHILIPPIANS 4:8
>
>I PETER 5:7
>
>JOEL 2:25
>
>I PETER 3:1-7
>
>I JOHN 1:8-9
>
>I JOHN 2:15-17
>
>JAMES 4:4-5

Alcoholism

They promise them freedom,
while they themselves are slaves of depravity—
for a man is a slave to whatever has mastered him.

2 PETER 2:19

■ ■ ■ ■

C heryl often asked me to pray for her. But whenever I asked her why, she would only say, "I'm going through a downer." What she didn't want me—or anyone else—to know about was her struggle with alcohol. Like most alcoholics, she lived in continuous denial that she was addicted to something that was tearing her life apart.

Finally, I confronted Cheryl and asked if she were, as I suspected, addicted to alcohol. She couldn't bring herself to use the word "addicted." Instead, she admitted only, "I have a slight problem in that area sometimes."

A controversy rages over whether addiction to alcohol is a "disease" or sin. Let's be clear on one thing. Addiction to anything apart from Jesus Christ is sin. It's true that almost any addiction may make a person sick. But to excuse drunkenness and whitewash it by calling it a "disease" is to minimize it and almost deny the problem exists.

If drunkenness is a "sickness," it's the only disease:

- that is contracted by an act of the will;
- that requires a license for distribution;
- that is bottled and sold;

- that requires outlets for its sale;
- that produces revenue for the government;
- that promotes crime;
- that is habit-forming;
- that is promoted by untold millions of dollars of advertising;
- for which we are fined and imprisoned when we exhibit its adverse symptoms;
- which produces thousands of deaths on our highways each month;
- which has no bacterial or viral cause, and for which there is no corrective medicine.

You may be saying, "How do I know whether I'm really addicted to alcohol, or I just like to drink?"

Many years ago a man who had been delivered from drunkenness traveled across this country lecturing on the evils of alcohol. He told me ten simple questions to ask to find out if someone is really addicted. If you answer yes to one of the questions, you may be an addict; if you answer yes to any two, you probably are addicted to alcohol; if you answer yes to three or more, you definitely are an alcoholic.

1. Do I crave a drink at a specific time each day?
2. Do I gulp my drinks and sneak extras?
3. Do I drink to relieve feelings of inadequacy?
4. Do I drink to escape worry and to dispel the blues?
5. Do I drink when overly tired in order to "get a grip?"
6. Is drinking affecting my peace of mind?
7. Is drinking making my home life unhappy?
8. Do I prefer to drink alone?
9. Do I require a drink the "next morning"?
10. Do I miss time at work or am I ineffective on the job because of my drinking?

Many excuse their propensity for drunkenness by saying it doesn't hurt anyone but themselves. But is this really true?

As I write this, I have just finished reading a news report about anti-nuclear power plant protesters in my state. They take their cause very seriously. But isn't alcoholism a much greater threat to our safety?

What if sixty or seventy people were killed daily by malfunctioning nuclear power plants? What if such problems seriously injured 1,500 people daily? What if the presence of nuclear power plants caused another 250 people to suffer permanent brain damage daily? What if the existence of those power plants caused fifteen people to commit suicide every day? What if it caused from 1,500 to 3,500 parents to abuse their children every day? What if it caused $35 billion a year in damages?

Our federal government would outlaw nuclear power plants immediately!

Yet the above tells the story of damage caused by alcohol—and not only is it not outlawed, it is seen as a good source of a large tax base for local, state, and federal governments.

How low have we slipped? A full decade ago we already knew alcohol was a leading cause of 50 percent of all automobile fatalities, 80 percent of all home violence, 60 percent of all child abuse, and 30 percent of all suicides.

So, there is no way drinking can be justified by a believer. If you find yourself addicted to alcohol and you've never accepted Jesus Christ as your Savior, that's the first step. No human power can set you free, only the divine power that comes by trusting Jesus Christ as your Savior (see chapter 9).

If you are a Christian and you're struggling in this area, there is wonderful hope for you. Jesus Christ already lives within you. His power and love can set you free from the bondage to drink!

COUNSEL FROM GOD'S WORD

Steps that will set you free from alcoholism:

1. Admit that drunkenness is sin, not just a social problem.

God's Word says, "Wine is a mocker, and beer a brawler; whoever is led astray by them is not wise" (Proverbs 20:1). Solomon also observed:

Who has woe? Who has sorrow? Who has strife? Who has complaints? Who has needless bruises? Who has bloodshot eyes? Those who linger over wine, who go to sample bowls of mixed wine. Do not gaze at wine when it is red, when it sparkles in the cup, when it goes down smoothly! In the end it bites like a snake and poisons like a viper. Your eyes will see strange sights, and your mind imagine confusing things (Proverbs 23:29-33).

The New Testament certainly isn't silent about the sin of drunkenness. The apostle Paul states clearly: "Do not get drunk on wine, which leads to debauchery" (Ephesians 5:18a).

Don't rationalize your drinking away and produce excuses about why you can't help yourself. The quicker you acknowledge that getting drunk is a sin against God and others, the quicker you can be delivered.

2. Decide now to never drink alcoholic beverages again. Don't try to 'taper' off slowly.

God wants you to walk away from alcoholism now and decide to never drink again. You may feel you're too weak to make that commitment, but it can be done. Remember, you have almighty God and His Word to back you up!

Don't forget that we "can do everything through him who gives [us] strength" (Philippians 4:13). The Lord promises, "Never will I leave you and never will I forsake you" (Hebrews 13:5b). No matter how bad your problem is, God invites you to "Call to me and I will answer you and tell you great and unsearchable things you do not know" (Jeremiah 33:3).

God has promised to provide His presence and His power for you to forsake this sin.

3. Establish new friends and relationships.

One reason many cannot stop drinking is that all the friends they keep drink. If that's true for you, seek immediately to establish acquaintances and build friendships with teetotalers, so the temptation to drink when you're with others won't occur. Scripture warns: "Do not be misled. Bad company corrupts good character" (1 Corinthians 15:33).

4. Become accountable to a group of godly people and meet regularly with them.

"Iron sharpens iron." It makes a positive difference when we have someone to whom to report weekly, someone who is willing to ask us the hard questions. Elisha had Elijah, Timothy had Paul. You need someone too.

James tells us to "confess your sins to each other and pray for each other so that you may be healed" (James 5:16a).

5. Remember that if for some reason you slip and drink again, God's grace is adequate and His forgiveness is available.

God won't erase the consequences of our failure and sin, but 1 John 1:9 tells us God is faithful and just and will forgive our sins. Even in our times of greatest discouragement, the Lord says to us: "My grace is sufficient for you, for my power is made perfect in weakness" (2 Corinthians 12:9). That's a great and reassuring promise of God for you.

6. Remind yourself daily why it's wrong for you to drink.

Alcoholism is wretched. Never forget that:
- it harms your body;
- it makes you a slave;
- it is poor stewardship of your time, money, and health;
- it may cause another believer to fall into sin;
- it dishonors the Holy Spirit who has made your body His temple (1 Corinthians 3:16);
- it supports an industry whose product brings poverty and death.

■ ■ ■ ■ ■

More biblical counsel

1 CORINTHIANS 6:9-10
ROMANS 14:21
PROVERBS 23:20
2 CORINTHIANS 5:17
JOHN 8:36
1 CORINTHIANS 10:13
PROVERBS 28:13
ISAIAH 26:3
MATTHEW 11:28
GALATIANS 5:22-23

Anger

A fool gives full vent to his anger,
but a wise man keeps himself under control.
PROVERBS 29:11

■ ■ ■ ■ ■

To most people, Carla and Teel looked like a better than average, church-going couple. Both were very attractive and seemed totally suited for each other. In their late twenties, they had been married about five years.

It wasn't until one Wednesday afternoon that Carla confided that she and Teel were separating from each other. His violent temper was completely out of control. In the past, Carla had always been able to cover her bruises and lacerations with makeup, but this Wednesday the bruises were too dark and the cuts too deep to hide anymore.

Teel had a hidden side that covered an abusive anger which expressed itself in horrible verbal assaults, slaps, and punches.

Perhaps, like Teel, in your anger you have become physically abusive. (If so, see chapter 3 on Abusive Behavior.)

Many people who aren't necessarily physically abusive make life miserable for those around them through their cutting words and lack of patience. In fact, almost everyone struggles with anger from time to time.

Only a few pages into God's Word, the first major case of anger erupted: "Then the Lord said to Cain, 'Why are you angry? Why is your face downcast?'" (Genesis 4:6). Sadly, Cain's misdirected anger ran its course, and shortly thereafter he struck down his brother, Abel.

If you've struggled with anger, it may surprise you to know that anger is not necessarily sinful behavior.

For example, when Saul learned that the Ammonites were threatening to take over the city of Jabesh, "the Spirit of God came upon him in power and he burned with anger" (1 Samuel 11:6b). That anger, you recall, brought victory for Israel and defeat for the enemies of God!

Jesus became angry when He saw the Temple being desecrated (John 2:17). The gospels also report that at the synagogue one Sabbath, the Pharisees opposed the healing of a handicapped man, and Jesus "looked around at them in anger" (Mark 3:5).

So, biblically, you can't say that anger *per se* is sin, since the Bible clearly says Jesus was without sin.

Also, Paul told the Ephesian believers, "In your anger, do not sin" (Ephesians 4:26). While not all anger is sin, it easily can become sin if we harbor resentment and bitterness, or "let the sun go down while [we] are still angry."

Anger becomes sin when it's directed at other people, when it's full of vindictiveness and retaliation, and when it is used as a crowbar to manipulate other people.

If anger dominates and clearly controls your life, follow these steps from God's Word.

COUNSEL FROM GOD'S WORD

1. Realize that it's fruitless to try to "pay back" others for wrongs they've perpetrated against you.

Since most of our anger is directed toward people who have offended us, we need to know what God says concerning our response.

> Do not take revenge, my friends, but leave room for God's wrath,
> for it is written: "It is mine to avenge; I will repay," says the Lord
> (Romans 12:19).

See also: Proverbs 6:34, 14:17, 12:16, and 14:29.

2. Understand that your wrath toward others blocks God's ministry to them.

While the object of your vented anger is dealing with how to respond, he or she cannot become the righteous person God desires. Your anger is blocking that. Your anger throws a monkey wrench into what God wants to do in that person's life—let alone what He wants to do in and through *your* life.

> My dear brothers, take note of this: Everyone should be quick to listen, slow to speak and slow to become angry, for man's anger does not bring about the righteous life that God desires (James 1:19-20).

3. Remember that being mad at others is a prelude to deeper disaster.

Proverbs warns that "stirring up anger produces strife" (Proverbs 30:33b) and that "starting a quarrel is like breaching a dam; so drop the matter before a dispute breaks out" (Proverbs 17:14). See also: Proverbs 25:28, 29:22; Ecclesiastes 7:9; and Matthew 5:22.

4. Recognize that God wants you to get rid of destructive anger.

We don't have to guess at what God wants from us in this area. The apostle Paul candidly says: "Get rid of all bitterness, rage and anger, brawling and slander" (Ephesians 4:31a).

If that's not clear enough, Paul says it again: "But now you must rid yourselves of all such things as these: anger, rage, malice, slander, and filthy language from your lips" (Colossians 3:8).

5. Before another day goes by, anger-proof your speech.

Have you done an inventory on your tone of voice and choice of words when talking to others at whom you are angry? Remember, volatile words are the prelude to volatile acts.

God's Word warns we will be judged by our speech:

> But I tell you that men will have to give account on the day of judgment for every careless word they have spoken (Matthew 12:36).

I'm glad to say that through some good biblical discipling, Teel finally faced his violent anger and temper as *sin*, not just a personality quirk. He went through some healing repentance, and through obedience to God's Word, left behind his life of misdirected anger.

Not only was Carla and Teel's marriage saved, it has become strong! At the head of that marriage today stands a tough, yet tender husband.

God can give you victory in this area, too! Make this your prayer:

> *Lord, I relinquish my anger to you right now. I renounce my bitterness, my rage, and all the burning hatred I've had for others. Lord, replace my anger with your sweet calm and love. Amen.*

■ ■ ■ ■ ■

More biblical counsel

COLOSSIANS 4:6
PROVERBS 10:11
PROVERBS 10:20
PROVERBS 12:18
PROVERBS 15:4
PROVERBS 16:21
PROVERBS 28:13
GALATIANS 5:23
LUKE 6:29
EPHESIANS 4:26

Backsliding

Therefore, my dear friends, stand firm.
Always give yourselves fully to the work of the Lord,
because you know that your labor in the Lord is not in vain.

I CORINTHIANS 15:58

■ ■ ■ ■ ■

Across the table sat a man with despair written all over his face. He recounted his losses from gambling, while sipping a drink from the bar, the epitome of a man who had hit rock bottom. No one would have ever guessed that only a year earlier this same man had attended church three times weekly, led a small home group, sung in a music group, and completed a course in lifestyle evangelism. On top of that, he was active on his church's missions board and had been planning to go into the mission field.

What happened? He became a backslider. His life and behavior looked no different from that of many defeated, discouraged, despairing unbelievers. The contrast between his condition and his former Christian lifestyle was stark indeed.

In some ways, it appeared as if this former church-goer had never known Christ personally. His Bible had been shelved for months and his prayer closet had not been used for close to a year. His tithing had dried up, as had his interest in spiritual things.

When I see such a person, I know one of two things is true. Either he or she never made a genuine commitment to Jesus Christ to begin with and was never born again, but only went through the motions, or he or she was truly born again, but is experiencing a temporary lapse in spiritual consciousness.

If a person is in the latter condition, how does he or she get that way, and how does this person get out?

WHY DO REAL CHRISTIANS BACKSLIDE?

Why does a person who at one time was turned on to Christ, who was full of zeal and love for the Lord and His Word, turn his or her back on it all and indulge in a sinful lifestyle?

1. Inconsistencies seen in other Christians.

Many people fall away from a close walk with the Lord because of the poor example they perceive in others. Someone they deeply respect for their spiritual maturity may be caught in a sin, or in some other way reveal he or she lives beneath the high standard of a committed Christian.

The observer can become disillusioned, discrediting the faith by reasoning, "If so and so did what he did, and he was supposedly a strong Christian, Christianity must not work." So this person slowly but surely walks away from the Lord, just like the one who caused him or her to stumble.

This is why the Bible states, "Be careful...that the exercise of your freedom does not become a stumbling block to the weak" (1 Corinthians 8:9). Though we have freedom in Christ, the welfare of the weaker brother or sister takes precedence over our rights.

Paul even applied this principle to the eating of foods: "Therefore, if what I eat causes my brother to fall into sin, I will never eat meat again, so that I will not cause him to fall" (1 Corinthians 8:13).

If your Christian walk has been damaged because of the negative example of another, don't forget that we can't determine our course of action on the basis of the behavior of others.

You and I must keep our eyes on Jesus alone as our high and holy example. "Let us fix our eyes on Jesus, the author and perfecter of our faith" (Hebrews 12:2). Only then will we never be disappointed.

2. Missing fellowship and worship with other believers.

Most backsliding initially starts by missing church. In my friend's life, it began by missing the Sunday evening service a lot. Pretty soon he didn't go to that service at all, staying home to watch television. Then he began missing Sunday morning service about once a month, then twice, and pretty soon consistently. He missed taking the Lord's Supper for three straight months. Along with that, he gave up his Bible study group, effectively cutting himself off from all fellowship.

Remember the biblical warning:

And let us consider how we may spur one another on toward love and good deeds. Let us not give up meeting together, as some are in the habit of doing, but let us encourage one another—and all the more as you see the Day approaching (Hebrews 10:24-25).

The illustration may be old but it's still true: If you take a coal from a bed of burning coals and set it aside, it will cool off while the other coals continue to burn. Why? That one coal was severed from its relationship with the others.

The same is true of us. Remove a Christian from fellowship and worship with other believers and—except for certain people in extraordinary circumstances—he or she will soon lose his or her warmth and zeal. It happens almost every time. We need each other!

If you are in a backslidden state and want to get out, get back to church, even if you don't feel like going.

3. The cessation of all financial giving.

A sure way to get into a backslidden state is to cease to give. Most people cease to give because they have become disinterested and lost their commitment.

The Scriptures teach a principle that few Christians realize: Commitment follows giving, it doesn't produce it. Jesus Himself said, "For where your treasure is, there your heart will be also" (Matthew 6:21).

Notice, Jesus did not say, "where your heart is, there your treasure will be," but "where your treasure is, there your heart will be also."

When a person stops giving, he or she cuts off the means of his or her commitment.

4. Compromise with the world.

Backsliding comes when, little by little, we begin to compromise with the world and its value system. There is ample warning in God's Word about this: "Do not love the world or anything in the world. If anyone loves the world, the love of the Father is not in him" (1 John 2:15).

When the Bible talks of the "world" here, it means that part of existence that is unregenerate, managed by the devil. We have to live in the world, but we are not to be of the world. We are not to become compatible with its ways and its values. We're not to develop a cozy friendship with it.

> You adulterous people, don't you know that friendship with the
> world is hatred toward God? Anyone who chooses to be a friend of
> the world becomes an enemy of God (James 4:4).

It can't be said any more clearly than that.

5. Backsliding results from not availing ourselves of God's provision.

Temptations come to one and all. The stronger we are in the Lord, the greater the temptations we will face. Temptation, however, is not sin. It's when we *yield* that sin begins. We don't have to yield. In fact, God has made a provision that most Christians forget about:

> No temptation has seized you except what is common to man. And
> God is faithful; he will not let you be tempted beyond what you
> can bear. But when you are tempted, he will also provide a way out
> so that you can stand up under it (1 Corinthians 10:13).

There are three promises contained in this wonderful verse.

First, everyone has temptations—you haven't been singled out. The "common to man" clause assures us of that.

Second, God's faithfulness prevents us from facing temptations stronger than we can bear. What a comforting truth to know, when the pressure to sin is bearing down on us.

Third, there is always a way out. God provides an out every time. We don't have to give in and yield to sin. Praise God!

COUNSEL FROM GOD'S WORD

If the things just listed cause backsliding, how does someone get out of such a condition? I believe God has given us several specific steps we need to follow in sequence.

1. Acknowledge to God that our hearts have grown cold.

Repentance and contrition are in order here. A time of refreshing will come immediately upon taking this step: "Repent, then, and turn to God, so that your sins may be wiped out, that times of refreshing may come from the Lord" (Acts 3:19).

This is a time to confess to God every known sin, and to realize that in His love and mercy He will forgive you. From now on, "strive always to keep [your] conscience clear before God and man" (Acts 24:16).

2. Turn to God in an act of contrition.

The prodigal son began his trek homeward by saying, "I will set out and go back to my father, and say to him: Father, I have sinned against heaven and against you. I am no longer worthy to be called your son" (Luke 15:18-19).

God esteems the person who humbly seeks the Lord in humility: "This is the one I esteem: he who is humble and contrite in spirit, and trembles at my word" (Isaiah 66:2b).

God greatly honors a humble and contrite heart. So if you've backslidden, seek the Lord and His mercy today. God's Word promises that if we seek the Lord with all our heart, we will find Him (Jeremiah 29:13).

3. Make any restitution you know you need to make.

Restitution is an essential prerequisite to restoration. Zaccheus said it best after he was converted to Christ:

Look, Lord! Here and now I give half of my possessions to the
poor, and if I have cheated anybody out of anything, I will pay back
four times the amount (Luke 19:8b).

God doesn't require you to pay back four-fold, but He does require full
restitution of whatever you've taken from someone else.

4. Find someone to whom you can be accountable.

Every Elisha needs his Elija, every Timothy needs his Paul, and you need
a strong brother or sister who will meet with you consistently to hold your feet
to the fire.

5. Return to church and Bible study immediately.

You may say, "But I don't have any desire to do that right now." It doesn't
matter whether the desire is there or not. A child has no desire to go to the den-
tist, but going will save his teeth.

Your obedience is what is important—the desire will come back following your renewed obedience. Remember the words of Scripture: "Those who
obey his commands live in him, and he in them" (1 John 3:24).

The Bible is clear in its teaching on obedience. We don't have to feel obedience in order to obey; we just have to obey. Remember again the words of
the apostle John:

This is how we know who the children of God are and who the
children of the devil are: Anyone who does not do what is right is
not a child of God (1 John 3:10a).

Notice something in that verse; it's not "feeling" what is right, but "doing"
what is right.

6. Begin immediately to memorize Scripture.

That may sound like poor counsel to a backslider. Why would a person
who has backslidden want to memorize Scripture? Again, it's not a question of
desire, but of obedience.

The Bible's words etched on our minds and spirits can and will do wonders to keep us from sin. That's why the psalmist said: "I have hidden your word in my heart that I might not sin against you" (Psalm 119:11).

The Bible tells us there is a definite connection between having God's Word in us and the amount of sin we commit. The more of His Word we have, the less we will sin or even want to sin.

7. Develop a prayer list and begin to pray.

Nothing can take the place of fellowship with God. Even if your daily prayer time is only three minutes, pray! I suggest designing your prayer list so that when your prayers are answered, you can thank God and mark them off. Even if you don't "feel" like praying, pray.

If you have been in a backslidden condition, remember that you haven't lost your salvation (see chapter 13, Doubting One's Salvation). But without repentance, you may very well go through some heavy discipline by the Lord, because the Bible says that He disciplines those whom He loves (Hebrews 12:6).

You might be interested in knowing about my backslidden friend. He deferred repentance and coming back for a few more months, but then became very ill. While in the hospital, he came back to the Lord in deep repentance, and soon thereafter began attending church again. Today he has a renewed love for God and His Word, and is active again in his local church.

God loves you and is waiting patiently for your return. Please get on your knees and pray this prayer:

Dear God, I confess to you that I have back-
slidden into sin. I confess my cold heart,
my disobedience, my rebellious spirit.
I ask for Your divine forgiveness and receive
it in Jesus' name. Have mercy on me as—in
repentance—I return to you. Amen.

· · · · ·

More biblical counsel

JAMES 5:19-20

COLOSSIANS 3:16-17

ISAIAH 55:7

1 JOHN 1:7-9

PROVERBS 3:5-6

ROMANS 8:37

2 CHRONICLES 7:14

PSALM 40:1-4

PSALM 51:12

PSALM 51:17

PROVERBS 28:13

HOSEA 10:12

HOSEA 14:1-2

AMOS 5:4-6

MICAH 7:18-19

ISAIAH 43:25

Bitterness

Be kind and compassionate to one another,
forgiving each other, just as in Christ God forgave you.
EPHESIANS 4:32

■ ■ ■ ■ ■

Phillip talked to me in the church parking lot for almost an hour. His face was drawn, his body gaunt. He confided that he was being treated for ulcerative colitis and exhaustion. He couldn't sleep more than a few hours a night and wondered why at age forty-one he felt seventy-one.

As I probed for the root cause of his problem, Phillip made it clear he had not had an adulterous affair or, in his opinion, committed any other major sin. He wasn't experiencing any economic problems, either. His business was booming. He and his wife had just moved into a beautiful new luxury home and taken their children to Disney World for two weeks.

But Phillip was "losing it" personally. The culprit? You guessed it. Bitterness.

Phillip had been fired from a very good job only seven years earlier. His boss, who owned the company, had been a good friend of his for years. Phillip felt the firing was unjust, even though it gave him the golden opportunity to go into business for himself, a move that caused him to greatly prosper financially.

As Phillip and I chatted in the parking lot, he finally confessed, with his head bowed and his body shaking, "I have harbored a grudge against John since the day I got my pink slip. In fact, I haven't spoken to him or his family for over seven years."

Phillip's bitter attitude was destroying his health, affecting his marriage, and moving him prematurely toward old age.

The blight of bitterness may be doing a number on your life, as well. It goes by many "aliases": animosity, grudge, resentment, fault-finding. Whatever the name, it all goes back to one thing: a refusal to release an offender from paying for a perceived offense.

Most bitter people feel justified in their bitterness. Outward bitterness confirms an inward "root of bitterness." The Bible sternly warns about this: "See to it that no one misses the grace of God, and that no bitter root grows up to cause trouble, and defile many" (Hebrews 12:15).

What is a "bitter root"? It always starts with a real or imagined offense brought on by another. It comes in various forms:

- Your character is assassinated.
- You're unjustly fired from your job.
- You're falsely accused of something you didn't do.
- You're cheated out of an inheritance.
- You got a "C" grade instead of a "B" or an "A."
- You were called an ugly name.
- Someone made a racial slur against you.
- You were made fun of by someone else.
- Someone lied about you, putting you in a bad light.
- You were a victim of age discrimination.
- You were robbed.
- You were raped.
- You were turned down because of bad credit.
- You were overcharged by a doctor or mechanic.
- You were cheated on by your spouse.
- Someone deliberately injured or murdered a loved one.
- Your spouse divorced you, against your wishes.
- Your fiancée broke off your engagement.
- A drunk driver totaled your car and injured you.

Such a list could go on for pages. But one thing is for sure. People wronged by others often feel it's their God-given right and duty to even the score. The problem, however, is that even after someone feels he or she has finally evened the score, the root of bitterness inside doesn't go away.

A RIGHT TO BE BITTER?

Do you and I ever really have a right to be bitter? Are bitterness and animosity ever justified?

Sooner or later, everyone in this life is offended or hurt by someone else. It comes with the turf, and you can't escape the hurt and pain that come when it happens. In one sense, we have no control whatever over what others do to us. But we do have control over how we ultimately respond to what others do.

Nursing a grudge ultimately hurts us worse than does the person who deeply offended us. Consider the devastating consequences of harboring bitterness:

1. It prevents acceptable worship.

The Lord Jesus Himself said:

Therefore if you are offering your gift at the altar, and there remember that your brother has something against you, leave your gift there in front of the altar. First go and be reconciled to your brother, then come and offer your gift (Matthew 5:23-24).

Yes, I know Jesus said, "if...your brother has something against you." But that doesn't let you or me off the hook if we have something against someone else. The principle is the same: We cannot offer acceptable worship to God as long as we allow an offense to fester between us and someone else. This means every time you go to church, it will be a struggle to worship as long as you're carrying around that grudge.

2. It affects God's forgiveness of your sins.

That's right! In the Sermon on the Mount, Jesus goes on to say:

> For if you forgive men when they sin against you, your heavenly
> Father will also forgive you. But if you do not forgive men their
> sins, your Father will not forgive your sins (Matthew 6:14-15).

It's impossible to walk in fellowship with God if you or I are harboring bitterness in our heart. Our refusal to forgive an offense by someone else blocks God's forgiveness of our own sins. God cannot and will not forgive an unforgiving heart. He's *not* saying Christians earn their forgiveness by forgiving others. But if we have truly received God's forgiveness, then we also must forgive others.

3. It makes you "greater" than God!

You may be saying, "You mean, harboring ill will against someone else elevates me above God? How?"

Consider this: If God is willing to humble Himself enough to forgive you of all your offenses, yet you refuse to forgive others of their offenses, then you are making yourself out to be someone higher and mightier than God!

Ludicrous?

That's absolutely right! Of course we're not greater than God. Thus, we have an obligation to forgive any and all who offend us. The apostle Paul says we are to forgive each other "just as in Christ God forgave you" (Ephesians 4:32).

In another epistle, Paul says: "Bear with each other and forgive whatever grievances you may have against one another. Forgive as the Lord forgave you" (Colossians 3:13).

4. It blocks your prayers.

In admonishing men to treat their wives kindly, Peter says:

> Husbands, in the same way be considerate as you live with your
> wives, and treat them with respect...so that nothing will hinder
> your prayers (1 Peter 3:7).

Wow! What a principle. If you turn that around, what Peter is saying is this: "If your prayers are being hindered, it could be because you are being inconsiderate with your wife." Harboring a grudge seriously damages our fellowship with God in prayer.

5. It confirms that you don't really love God.

In his first epistle, the apostle John writes: "If anyone says, 'I love God,' yet hates his brother, he is a liar" (1 John 4:20). Strong words! But John is right on target. Our refusal to forgive those whom we know here on earth cancels out our profession that we really love God in heaven.

6. It assumes a right we don't have.

Paul clearly says:

Do not take revenge, my friends, but leave room for God's wrath,
for it is written, "It is mine to avenge, I will repay" says the Lord
(Romans 12:19).

Revenge is God's department, not yours or mine. He will see that justice is done. That is not our business. For me to shove God aside and say, "Lord, I'm going to administer punishment in this particular situation" is to assume authority God never granted. It is, in fact, equivalent to "playing God."

If harboring bitterness is so personally devastating, why do we nurse grudges? We do it because we don't like being taken advantage of. We don't like others hurting us. We don't like being ignored, lied about, or put down. So we lash out in revenge, which only produces further heartache.

COUNSEL FROM GOD'S WORD

If you are nursing a grudge or feeling animosity toward someone, I challenge you to take the following steps immediately.

1. Confess to God that you have sinned by harboring bitterness in your soul.

No, this isn't an easy first step. We would much rather justify our actions before God based on the behavior of the one who hurt us. But until we acknowledge the sinfulness of our actions, we're only fooling ourselves. King

David discovered this firsthand: "When I kept silent [about my sin], my bones wasted away through my groaning all day long" (Psalm 32:3).

2. Ask others to pray that you will do the right thing.

James says in his epistle: "Therefore confess your sins to each other and pray for each other so that you may be healed" (James 5:16). As others pray for you, you will find it easier to go to step three.

3. Go to the person who offended you and verbally forgive him or her.

If the person who offended you knows you've nursed a grudge against him or her, go to that person and say: "I'm here today for two reasons. First, to ask for your forgiveness for harboring a grudge against you. Second, I'm here to say that I fully and freely forgive you for what I perceived to be an offense against me. I don't hold anything against you anymore."

This is a tough step to take, admittedly. You may be thinking, "But what if the other person doesn't accept my forgiveness?" That is their business and problem, not yours. You've done what God told you to do.

You also may be thinking, "But what if they do the same thing again? Do I have to forgive them a second time?" After reading these verses, you decide:

Then Peter came to Jesus and asked, "Lord, how many times shall I forgive my brother when he sins against me? Up to seven times?" Jesus answered, "I tell you, not seven times but seventy times seven" (Matthew 18:21-22).

That may not have been what Peter wanted to hear. But it goes further than that. Jesus was really saying that we're obligated to forgive in an unlimited way.

4. Remember that love forgives even the worst offenses.

Later in life, Peter himself could write: "Above all, love each other deeply because love covers over a multitude of sins" (1 Peter 4:8).

When Edwin Markham, the poet, came to his retirement years, the story is told, he discovered his banker had defrauded him of all his retirement funds.

In his bitterness, Markham could no longer write poetry. He became morose, sour, ineffective. Then one day, while doodling at his desk, he began to draw some circles. Convicted by the Holy Spirit, he penned these words:

> He drew a circle that shut me out,
> Heretic, rebel, a thing to flout;
> But love and I had the wit to win;
> We drew a circle that took him in!

Ah, the answer to bitterness: Draw a bigger circle! One that will take in the offender and thus repay evil with good.

Does it work? Ask Phillip. For seven long years, bitterness was eating him alive. After our conversation in the church parking lot, he went to his old boss and, in the spirit of John 13, washed his feet, humbling himself before him and verbally forgiving him. Later, Phillip told me, "I feel like I've been born again…again!"

If you are harboring resentment or nursing some grudge, pray this prayer:

> *Lord, I lay down this offense at your feet, confess my bitterness as sin, and ask for Your divine forgiveness. Give me wisdom as I go to the person who offended me. I pray for him and ask you to bless him this day. Amen.*

■ ■ ■ ■ ■

More biblical counsel

MATTHEW 18:23-35
EPHESIANS 4:31
1 PETER 2:23
ROMANS 12:18
PROVERBS 19:3
PROVERBS 26:24-26
JAMES 4:10

Depression

"When you pass through the waters, I will be with you;
and when you pass through the rivers, they will not sweep over you.
When you walk through the fire, you will not be burned;
the flames will not set you ablaze.
For I am the Lord,
your God, the Holy One of Israel, your Savior..."
ISAIAH 43:2-3

■ ■ ■ ■ ■

Stories about depression don't always have a happy ending. "A man's spirit sustains him in sickness," King Solomon observed many centuries ago, "but a crushed spirit, who can bear?" (Proverbs 14:18).

Perhaps nothing is heavier than the cumbersome cloud of dark depression that descends upon some people. Such a spirit of depression is no respecter of persons. It comes upon young, middle-aged, and elderly. It visits rich and poor, educated and uneducated, professional and non-professional, male and female, married and single alike. Sometimes even strong, Bible-believing Christians experience dark periods of depression.

Left unchecked, depression is life-threatening. Virtually all suicides result from sudden or prolonged bouts of deep depression.

Depression is a mood marked by sadness and gloom—sometimes appearing for no apparent reason—which produces unusual disinterest in life and sometimes a deep sense of despair.

The symptoms of depression are not hard to detect:
- Loss of appetite
- Loss of sleep
- Inordinate fatigue
- Overindulgence in food, beverage, or sleep
- Disinterest in life in general
- Hypochondria (always whining or complaining about some real or imagined physical ailment)
- Unkempt appearance
- Occasional loss of sex drive
- Loss of any drive to achieve
- Unexplained crying spells
- Feelings of heaviness and oppression
- Extremely negative self-image
- Anti-social behavior (including withdrawal from people)
- Lack of long-range plans
- Oversensitivity

If these are the symptoms, what are some of the causes of this dark spirit of gloom and despair?

CAUSES OF DEPRESSION

I. Physical causes

Occasionally a person will experience extreme depression because of a change in his or her physical well-being. In women, for example, hormonal imbalance can bring about a spirit of depression. This often can be treated with estrogen, and women need to consult their physician to see if this is at the root of their emotional downturn.

In both men and women, prolonged illnesses or traumatic injuries can bring on depression. Diabetes caused one man I knew to lose both his legs. While recovering in a Veteran's hospital, he attempted suicide; the attempt was thwarted, thanks to a quick-thinking orderly. In a note, this man had written: "I have nothing to live for if I can't stand on my own two feet."

Certainly Job fought depression over his physical pain when he wrote:

...So I have been allotted months of futility, and nights of misery
have been assigned to me. When I lie down, I think "how long
before I get up?" My body is clothed with worms and scabs, my
skin is broken and festering (Job 7:3-5).

This is but one biblical case where depression came as a result of a physical problem. While both Scripture and experience indicate that physical defor-
mities and illness may bring on depression, usually there are other reasons.

2. Unresolved guilt

Please take note of the word "unresolved." Guilt, in and of itself, is not a
bad thing. It's a built-in alarm God has placed within us that goes off when
we've sinned. Such guilt is good because it drives us to repentance, and thus to
wholeness. But if guilt is unresolved, or covered up with pseudo guilt
removers, depression is sure to move in and set up shop.

Guilt is to the soul what fever is to the body. Fever, though it causes dis-
comfort, sounds a "wake-up call" to the body alerting it that it has been invaded
by something which doesn't belong. Similarly, guilt is God's wake-up call that
an enemy has invaded the soul and spirit. If we refuse to take action (repent),
guilt wreaks havoc in our lives.

David experienced this after he sinned against Bathsheba:

When I kept silent, my bones wasted away through my groaning all
day long. For day and night your hand was heavy upon me; my
strength was sapped as in the heat of summer. Then I acknowledged my sin to you, and did not cover up my iniquity (Psalm
32:3-5a).

Persistence in sin with no remorse, no contrition, and no repentance will
bring a spirit of depression that won't let us go.

3. The loss of a loved one

Normal grief follows the loss of a parent, spouse, child, or close friend.
Mary's comment to Jesus drips with grief: "If you had been here my brother

would not have died" (John 11:21). When He went to the tomb, Jesus Himself wept. But sometimes long after the normal period of grieving has passed, waves of depression come back to constrict the survivor.

Grief is one thing, but lingering grief turns into depression of the spirit. I know a woman whose husband has been dead for nearly two years, yet she still finds herself depressed and in a spirit of despair most of the time.

4. Boredom

Some depression is brought on by what appears to be inescapable boredom. Life becomes a "hum-drum" affair for some. This ailment afflicts all classes of society, not just the poor. Solomon talked about this kind of existence when he wrote:

A man may have a hundred children and live many years; yet no matter how long he lives, if he cannot enjoy his prosperity and does not receive a proper burial, I say that a still-born child is better off than he (Ecclesiastes 6:3).

How tragic to be prosperous and live to a ripe old age, only to die a miserable death having never found fulfillment and meaning in life. Many people who are depressed because of boredom in their lives have not learned to wisely invest their lives into the lives of others.

5. Direct attack from the enemy of our souls

Satan brings attacks of depression upon believers and non-believers alike, through various means. In the Bible, we find King Saul repeatedly trying to kill David because of jealous rage. We're told that during such fits, "an evil spirit from God came forcefully upon Saul" (1 Samuel 18:10).

In this case, God allowed an evil and demonic spirit from the devil to enrage Saul. Saul's anger and jealousy led to his deep depression. Similarly, Jonah became extremely depressed when his anger got the best of him. Whether Satan attacks through anger, jealousy, rage, or revenge, the result is always the same. Such attacks leave us depressed.

6. Self-pity

"Pity parties" often lead to depression. Moses experienced this while dealing with God about the troublesome nation of Israel:

> "Why have you brought this trouble on your servant? What have I
> done to displease you that you put the burden of all these people
> on me?... If this is how you are going to treat me, put me to death
> right now" (Numbers 11:11, 15).

When we wallow in self-pity, depression is sure to follow. Elijah felt this way when Jezebel threatened to kill him. Elijah fled into the wilderness, collapsed under a tree in despair, then cried out to God: "I have had enough, Lord," he said, "Take my life; I am no better than my ancestors" (1 Kings 19:4).

If such outstanding men of God as Elijah, Moses, and Job went through times of depression, there's hope for us.

COUNSEL FROM GOD'S WORD

What is the cure for depression? Again, let's look to the Bible for guidance.

1. Acknowledge the source of your depression.

Since Jesus came to give us life to the full (John 10:10), and since every good and perfect gift is from God (James 1:17), it's obvious who the ultimate source of depression is.

As the accuser of the brethren, Satan wants you to feel badly, think badly, act badly, and be convinced that there is no way out—that you're trapped in your depression. The devil will do all in his limited power to take your unpleasant circumstances and use them as a source and means of depression in your life.

But it's not enough to acknowledge the source of one's depression. Several more crucial steps must be taken.

2. Claim what you have.

Many times, when we're deep in the pits, we tend to forget who we are and what we have in Christ. Remember, you're a child of God, the apple of His eye, His heir, and the One on whom He has promised to lavish His love. You have it all! If your depression seems to loom as the largest thing in your life, remember, "the one who is in you is greater than the one in the world" (1 John 4:4b).

What a promise! What a comfort! The power and presence of Jesus Christ inside you is greater and more powerful than any spirit of depression. As the object of God's care and concern, you can rest assured that your well-being is His highest priority. "You can throw the whole weight of your anxieties on Him, for you are his personal concern" (1 Peter 5:7, Phillips).

God is more than powerful enough to handle whatever is causing your depression.

3. Give your depression over to God.

King David once confessed to the Lord:

My heart is in anguish within me; the terrors of death assail me.
Fear and trembling have beset me, horror has overwhelmed me. I
said, "O, if I had the wings of a dove! I would flee away and stay in
the desert, I would hurry to my place of shelter, far from the tem-
pest and storm" (Psalm 55:4-8).

In his despair, David wanted to run. You can run, all right, but you can-not hide from your problems. Many people with depression think a change of scenery would help their depression to disappear. But all that does is rearrange it. Sometimes, too much change only aggravates the situation.

It's better by far to officially hand your depression over to God, much as a traveler hands his or her luggage over to a skycap. "Cast your cares on the Lord, and he will sustain you" (Psalm 55:22a).

I've found it's best to verbally speak as you offer your situation over to the Lord. Find a place, make a time, and write it down, so that you will be able to say, "At that place, in that month, on that day, at that time, I relinquished my depression over to God." You may want to say something like this:

Lord, I hereby relinquish all my depression to you. I know it doesn't belong in my life, and you're not the author of it, so I hand it all over to you and ask that I never receive it back again. Amen.

4. Worship and praise God with great intensity.

This is the last thing a depressed person feels like doing, but it's a vital step to take, nonetheless.

During the days of Babylonian captivity, God's people were in a severe state of depression. They said:

By the rivers of Babylon we sat and wept when we remembered Zion. There on the poplars we hung our harps.... How can we sing the songs of the Lord while in a foreign land? (Psalm 137:1, 4).

Good question! How can we sing the songs of the Lord while in a state of depression? It isn't easy, but it's essential! Praise and worship lift depression faster than anything else. The Bible teaches that praise and worship are like a divine lever, prying the spirit of depression off our back and shoulders.

For all who mourn and grieve, the Lord wants to:

...Bestow on them a crown of beauty instead of ashes, the oil of gladness instead of mourning, and a garment of praise instead of a spirit of despair (Isaiah 61:3).

There it is! God wants to replace our spirit of despair with "a garment of praise"! The presence of praise produces the absence of depression. Men of God, like Jonah, Jehoshaphat, and Paul, all experienced this. You can, too! Victory comes as a result of praise.

5. Start serving others in ministry.

You may be thinking, "Aren't you getting the cart before the horse? Shouldn't I wait until I'm completely over this depression before I try to help other people?" No! All of us are called on to "serve one another." Part of the way God lifts your depression is allowing you to serve others. But there's still one more step.

6. Get into the habit of continually giving thanks to God.

True, it's hard to give thanks when you're "down." Yet this is the very time we need to thank God. Ephesians 5:20 says we're to give thanks "for everything." In 1 Thessalonians 5:18, we're commanded to give thanks "in all circumstances." Why? "For this is God's will for you in Christ Jesus."

Make this your prayer:

Lord, I would never have asked for these circumstances, but I thank you for them. Teach me what you want me to learn through them. Amen.

■ ■ ■ ■ ■

More biblical counsel

> PSALM 16
>
> PSALM 12
>
> PSALM 42
>
> PSALM 30:5B
>
> 2 CHRONICLES 20:20-28
>
> 2 CORINTHIANS 4:17
>
> ISAIAH 49:9-11
>
> JEREMIAH 29:13-14
>
> NEHEMIAH 8:10
>
> PSALM 37:4
>
> PSALM 77
>
> PSALM 121:3-8
>
> ISAIAH 26:3
>
> ISAIAH 53:4-5
>
> PROVERBS 3:5-6
>
> PSALM 38:1-4
>
> PSALM 38:21-22
>
> PSALM 23
>
> PSALM 56

Divorce and Remarriage

So guard yourself in your spirit,
and do not break faith with the wife of your youth.
MALACHI 2:15

■ ■ ■ ■ ■

From all appearances, Bill and Tonya weren't that much different from any other young American couple. They had been married eleven years and had two children, ages nine and six. Bill was an auto mechanic; Tonya worked part-time at a local dry cleaners in the evening. Both attended church fairly regularly. They weren't super-saints, but who is? Then, one day, Bill moved out of the house and into an apartment with a single buddy of his.

The problem? Bill came home, ate his dinner, fell asleep on the couch nightly, and paid Tonya little or no attention when she got home from work, except when he wanted sex. In response, she pulled away from him emotionally. Bill, in turn, lost all feelings for Tonya. All they still had in common was that they were married on the same day and lived under the same roof. Everything else was gone. Angry, frustrated, lonely, and stubborn, Bill felt his marriage to Tonya was all but over. In the end, she filed for divorce.

Divorce! In one sense the word is worse than death. In another sense it has become such a common word, some don't even bat an eye when it is spoken.

WHAT CAUSES DIVORCE?

Ask a group of divorced men and women what caused their divorce, and you often will hear, "My spouse and I drifted apart and lost touch with each other, and soon had nothing in common." Oh, divorcees may use different words, but the gist is frequently the same. One woman recently put it this way: "Somehow that which attracted us to each other now repels us."

Why the complete change of heart? Many reasons could be listed. Here are a few:

- Lack of communication
- Alcohol
- Debt
- Infidelity
- Uncontrolled anger
- Different interests
- In-laws
- Different sexual expectations
- Insensitivity
- Boredom
- Stubbornness
- Lying
- Instability
- Physical abuse

The reasons are endless, but in reality there is only one reason—a refusal on the part of either husband or wife, or both, to carry out their "role" in marriage.

THE HUSBAND'S ROLE

The man's role can be summed up in one sentence: "Husbands, love your wives, just as Christ loved the church" (Ephesians 5:25). Paul goes on in that chapter to explain what kind of love he's talking about.

1. It's a sacrificial love.

The Bible says that Christ "gave himself up for her" (Ephesians 5:25). This means a husband should go to any length and breadth to love his wife— even giving his life for hers, if need be.

2. It's a cleansing love.

Christ loved the church, "cleansing her by the washing with water through the word" (Ephesians 5:26). This means a husband should do all in his power to protect the purity of his wife.

3. It's a nourishing love.

The Bible says, "no one ever hated his own body, but he feeds and cares for it, just as Christ does the church" (Ephesians 5:29). Similarly, as the leader in his home, the husband is to spiritually nourish his wife.

4. It's a caring kind of love.

Paul also says he "cares." A wife can live without a lot of things, but not without knowing where she stands in her husband's value system. First, he must wholeheartedly love the Lord. Then, he must cherish his wife.

When a husband neglects or refuses to fulfill his God-given responsibilities, he ends up downgrading his wife. He leaves her feeling unloved, unprotected, vulnerable, spiritually deprived, and uncared for. Believe me, no woman can long live that way.

THE WIFE'S ROLE

Her role also can be summed up in one sentence: "Wives, submit to your husbands as to the Lord" (Ephesians 5:22).

This command suggests there is a hierarchy within marriage, as in most of life. The Bible goes on to state that the husband is the head of the wife, as Christ is the head of the church.

Submission does not mean a wife must subject herself to anything her husband asks her to do. She has no obligation to "submit" to his demands if those demands are contrary to God's Word. Nor does submission mean a wife cannot express her opinion. In contrast to Pilate (Matthew 27:19), a wise husband listens to the counsel of his wife.

Submission means a woman acknowledges her husband as the God-ordained head of their union. It means that ultimately God has called the husband to make the final decision in matters pertaining to the marriage.

In a healthy marriage, the husband rarely overrides his wife's counsel, wishes, or advice. Instead, he seeks what's best for her, for them, and for the family as a whole. In any other area of life, a good leader does the same thing.

But admittedly not all marriages are healthy. If one or both spouses are failing to carry out their God-given roles, is divorce inevitable? Is it even an option?

HOW GOD VIEWS DIVORCE

Scripture is clear about what God thinks: "'I hate divorce,' says the Lord God of Israel" (Malachi 2:16). Those words don't even need to be interpreted. God hates any attempt to break the covenant of two He has joined together.

Jesus taught the permanence of marriage as well. When the Pharisees tested Jesus by asking Him if it were lawful for a man to divorce his wife, Jesus told them:

> "Moses permitted you to divorce your wives because your hearts
> were hard. But it was not this way from the beginning. I tell you
> that anyone who divorces his wife, except for marital unfaithful-
> ness, and marries another woman commits adultery" (Matthew
> 19:8-9).

It is interesting to me how Jesus took the religious leaders of His day right back to God's original plan for marriage. Originally, it was to be a permanent "until death do us part" covenant relationship. There was no provision for divorce. Moses eventually gave instructions about divorce because men *were* divorcing their wives, contrary to God's wishes.

God's original plan is outlined for us in the book of beginnings, Genesis: "For this reason a man will leave his father and mother and be united to his wife, and they will become one flesh" (Genesis 2:24).

In the New Testament, both Jesus and the apostle Paul used this same verse when they taught about the permanence of marriage. Paul also makes it clear:

> To the married I give this command (not I, but the Lord): a wife
> must not separate from her husband...And a husband must not
> divorce his wife (1 Corinthians 7:10-11).

These and other passages make it clear that God's will is that once the marriage bond has been established, it is not to be broken.

GROUNDS FOR DIVORCE (AND REMARRIAGE)

But the question is often asked: "Does God prohibit divorce altogether? Aren't there some circumstances under which God's Word permits divorce?"

Yes, in two instances Scripture teaches that divorce may be permissible. The first is the sexual unfaithfulness of one's spouse, whether heterosexual or homosexual infidelity.

> "But I tell you that anyone who divorces his wife, except for marital unfaithfulness, causes her to become an adulteress, and anyone who marries the divorced woman commits adultery" (Matthew 5:32).

The term "adultery" refers to a married man or woman having sex with someone other than his or her spouse. This is referred to as the "exception" clause.

Please understand that Jesus is not commanding you to divorce if your spouse has committed adultery. As a Christian, you must forgive him or her and you may opt not to divorce, especially if your spouse repents.

In other words, adultery doesn't automatically sever the marriage relationship, though it blemishes it severely. Jesus said essentially the same thing:

> "I tell you that anyone who divorces his wife, except for marital unfaithfulness, and marries another woman, commits adultery" (Matthew 19:9).

Jesus permitted divorce in cases of sexual unfaithfulness, but in no way did He say divorce is an automatic given.

The second area where divorce is permitted is when one's non-Christian partner decides to exit the marriage.

> But if the unbeliever leaves, let him do so. A believing man or woman is not bound in such circumstances; God has called us to live in peace (1 Corinthians 7:15).

This means if a person is married to an unbeliever, and the unbelieving spouse decides to leave the marriage, and does so, the believing partner isn't "bound" to that marriage. Again, the verse is suggesting not that the believer *must* pursue divorce, but that he or she may if the situation isn't corrected.

Remember, the obligation to forgive and stand for your marriage takes precedence over your "right" to divorce your spouse. Having an unbelieving spouse is not, in itself, grounds for divorce. The Bible is clear here:

> If any brother has a wife who is not a believer and she is willing to
> live with him, he must not divorce her. And if a woman has a hus-
> band who is not a believer, and he is willing to live with her, she
> must not divorce him (1 Corinthians 7:12b-13).

From a Christian perspective, divorce is to be avoided at all costs, since God "hates divorce." Perhaps the following questions and answers can help clarify some of the issues revolving around divorce and remarriage.

Q. Besides my spouse committing adultery or my unbelieving spouse deserting me, under what other circumstances may I file for divorce?

A. Those are the only two reasons given in Scripture.

Q. But what if I'm the victim of ongoing physical abuse? Isn't that grounds for divorce?

A. Not biblically, but you do need to remove yourself from the situation and seek protection until your spouse has repented, forsaking his or her violent ways (see chapter 3, Abusive Behavior).

Q. May a divorced person remarry?

A. Yes, if you were divorced because your spouse would not repent of his or her ongoing sexual infidelity, or if your unbelieving spouse decided to desert you.

Q. What if my divorce wasn't on biblical grounds, but it was prior to my salvation? Am I free to remarry?

A. Yes, if your previous spouse has died or already remarried. If he or she hasn't remarried, reconciliation still may be possible. That you are a Christian now may actually increase the likelihood the two of you can be reconciled, especially if you were the one who initiated the divorce. Begin by seeking your ex-husband or ex-wife's forgiveness.

Q. *What if I got divorced before I was a Christian, married someone else, then became a Christian? Should I divorce my second spouse and go back to my first spouse, if he or she hasn't remarried?*

A. No, Scripture teaches you should make the best of the marriage you're in now (Deuteronomy 24:1-4). Leaving your second spouse to remarry your former spouse would dishonor the Lord. Two wrongs never make a right.

Q. *If I don't love my spouse anymore, isn't it wrong to remain married, even though I have no biblical grounds for divorce?*

A. It's never "wrong" to remain married, since marriage is a covenant between you, your spouse, and the Lord. Besides, love is a choice. You can learn to love your spouse again by doing loving things for him or her. "Feelings" of love will follow your obedience in this area.

CONSEQUENCES OF DIVORCE

Divorce never solves problems, but it sure creates a few. Consider these consequences of divorce:

1. It creates severe economic difficulties.

I have never known divorce to improve a couple's financial situation. Just the opposite. I recently asked a prominent attorney what an average divorce costs. He said before it's all over, it will cost half the price of an expensive new sports car! After the divorce, the economic impact is even more severe. The cost of maintaining two households is exorbitant. Often, the woman's standard of living plummets the worst.

2. It creates an "unprotected" species.

When a couple divorce, the woman no longer is under the God-ordained umbrella of protection her former husband was supposed to provide for her.

She becomes a "sitting duck" for the onslaughts of the world, the flesh, and the devil.

3. It plagues one's conscience.

A man who divorced his wife told me he still feels a sense of shame, guilt, and terrible disappointment in himself for initiating that divorce twenty-one years ago. Most divorcees feel a sense of ongoing shame. Even though God forgives any and all sin, the consequences of a divorce initiated on unbiblical grounds never end.

4. It sets a precedent for your children to someday divorce their spouses.

More than half of all couples filing for divorce today had at least one parent who ended his or her first marriage in divorce. Even though they know the pain of divorce firsthand, the children of divorce are more apt than others to end their own marriages in divorce. So the consequences of divorce affect generations to come.

5. It increases the probability of ongoing failure.

This doesn't mean that if you're divorced, you're doomed to a life of failure. But it is true that divorcees fail in other areas of life more frequently than non-divorced men and women.

6. It increases the chance of entering into a non-biblical marriage.

Studies indicate that people who go through a divorce are more likely than not to marry again. Most will enter into an unbiblical union. Significantly less than fifty percent of those marriages are likely to succeed.

7. It creates a horrible loneliness that can lead to sin.

Say what you will, but divorce brings a deep sense of loneliness, even for the person who initiated the divorce. If unchecked, loneliness can lead to immorality.

One man confessed to me that a divorce he did not want produced so much pain and loneliness that he pursued a new relationship much too quickly. That relationship, thought to be above-board in every way, led one

Friday night to sexual sin. Ashamed and guilt-ridden, this man ended up telling his own children that for the first time in his life, he had sex with someone who was not his wife. Why? It all began with divorce!

COUNSEL FROM GOD'S WORD

1. If your divorce isn't final yet:

Maybe as you read this, divorce proceedings are pending. If you have initiated those proceedings, withdraw them at once. "A wife must not separate from her husband. But if she does, she must remain unmarried, or else be reconciled to her husband. And a husband must not divorce his wife" (1 Corinthians 7:10-11). It is contrary to God's will to initiate divorce unless you have biblical grounds.

Solomon was right: "haste leads to poverty" (Proverbs 21:5).

Don't proceed rashly. Instead, ask your partner to forgive you for filing divorce papers, and withdraw them quickly.

2. If you are already divorced, and you and your spouse have not remarried:

The circumstances may look hopeless, but remember, you and God make a majority. On the basis of Ephesians 4:32, decide today to forgive your spouse, and ask him or her to forgive you. Remember, regardless of why you are divorced, God wants you to pursue reconciliation. "Do not repay anyone evil for evil" (Romans 12:17).

You may object, "But I don't have any feelings for my former spouse." Feelings have nothing to do with whether or not to obey the Lord. Do the godly thing!

3. If you are already divorced, your spouse has remarried, and you haven't:

If your divorce was a biblically allowed divorce, you are free to remarry, but only in the Lord (Matthew 19:3-9).

4. If you are already divorced and remarried, and your spouse hasn't remarried:

Do not divorce your spouse and return to your former spouse. That would only be adding sin to sin. Repent over your remarriage (if you weren't biblically eligible to remarry), then know God has forgiven you. Make the best out of your present marriage and put Christ in the center of it (Matthew 6:33).

5. If you are divorced, not yet remarried, and your divorce wasn't biblically allowed:

Do not marry someone else. That would be adultery (Mark 10:11). You have two choices. Either reconcile with your divorced spouse, or remain single (1 Corinthians 7:11ff).

6. If you are divorced, but you didn't want the divorce:

The question comes up, "Am I biblically eligible to remarry?" Even if you didn't want the divorce, God wants you to pursue reconciliation of that marriage. If and when your ex-spouse remarries, you are free to marry, but only another Christian.

If your marriage was broken by adultery, however, and the adulterer precipitated the divorce, you are free to remarry, in the Lord.

What about Bill and Tonya? Two wonderful things happened. After some biblical counsel, Tonya withdrew her divorce papers, realizing she had no biblical grounds. Through the counsel of a close friend, Bill learned what his biblical responsibilities were as a husband. He changed, he and Tonya were reconciled, and their marriage improved dramatically.

■ ■ ■ ■ ■

More biblical counsel

PROVERBS 18:22

ROMANS 7:1-2

1 CORINTHIANS 7

1 PETER 3:1-7

PHILIPPIANS 2:3-11

1 CORINTHIANS 13

EPHESIANS 5:22-32

PROVERBS 31

MARK 10:1-11
MATTHEW 5:31-32
COLOSSIANS 3:18-19
DEUTERONOMY 24:1-4
MATTHEW 6:5-15
JAMES 4:7-12

Doubting God's Word

Your word is a lamp to my feet
and a light for my path.
PSALM 119:105

■ ■ ■ ■ ■

Is the Bible the Word of God? Is it reliable? Is it authoritative by virtue of the fact that it is infallible? Can we really be sure it's inerrant? Is the Bible alone God's Word, or do we need additional documents to get a picture of the full record of God's revelation in Jesus Christ?

I'll call him Dirk. I met him at the local university campus after he had visited our church. Dirk was a brilliant young student majoring in microbiology. Affable and seemingly open, he was pleased I had come to see him.

I had the privilege of sharing the whole gospel story with Dirk. He seemed genuinely enthusiastic about hearing the message, and literally hung on every word I said as I told him about the death of Jesus Christ and His resurrection. I showed him what was required to receive Christ and asked him if he would like to do that.

Dirk looked down at the floor of his dorm room. "I can't accept Christ, because I'm not sure the Bible is really a true and reliable book. What if it has errors?"

Most of the arguments against the Bible being God's infallible Word fall into the following categories:

- The Bible contradicts known scientific facts. It contains phrases like, "to the ends of the earth." Everyone knows the earth is round, not flat, and has no "ends."
- The Bible contradicts itself, and thus can't be accurate and true.
- You can't take the Bible literally because some of its statements are culturally outdated. It says women should be in submission to their husbands, for instance. Everyone knows that was an accepted Eastern custom at the time, but that doesn't necessarily mean it's applicable in our culture today.
- The Bible has been copied and translated so many times and into so many languages, it's lost some of its truth in the process.

Well, is the Bible really reliable and adequate? Is it true from cover to cover? Or are we claiming something the Bible doesn't even claim for itself? Or worse, claiming something that doesn't stand up under scrutiny?

COUNSEL FROM GOD'S WORD

Most people who have problems accepting the Bible as fully inspired and reliable have never read the Bible, have prejudices against it based on what they've heard from critics, and certainly aren't acquainted with the Author.

What then is our basis for believing the Bible is indeed the Word of God?

I. The claims of the Bible itself.

Scripture certainly claims to be without error. In Proverbs 30:5 we read, "Every word of God is flawless." King David testified, "And the words of the Lord are flawless, like silver refined in a furnace of clay, purified seven times" (Psalm 12:6).

David also said that the "Law of the Lord is perfect" (Psalm 19:7). And again, "As for God, his way is perfect, the word of the Lord is flawless" (Psalm 18:30). The psalmist also could say, "Your word, O Lord, is eternal; it stands firm in the heavens" (Psalm 119:89).

When Jesus spoke of the Scriptures, He was speaking of the thirty-nine books of the Old Testament. He considered them inspired and authoritative: "It is easier for heaven and earth to disappear than for the least stroke of a pen to drop out of the law" (Luke 16:17).

Again making reference to the Old Testament writings, Jesus went on to say, "Scripture cannot be broken" (John 10:35).

The apostle Paul claimed: "All scripture is God-breathed, and is useful for teaching, rebuking, correcting, and training in righteousness" (2 Timothy 3:16).

In establishing the veracity and authority of the Bible, the apostle Peter said:

> No prophecy of Scripture came about by the prophet's own inter-
> pretation. For prophecy never had its origin in the will of man, but
> men spoke from God as they were carried along by the Holy Spirit
> (2 Peter 1:20b-21).

2. Fulfillment of prophecy.

The veracity of God's Word is further established by the accurate fulfill-ment of all its prophecies. Some three hundred Old Testament predictions found their fulfillment in Jesus Christ alone. They're hard to refute when you realize that all these prophecies were made hundreds of years before Christ was born. Let me list just a few:

- *Birth at Bethlehem* (Prophesied: Micah 5:2; Prophecy Fulfilled: Matthew 2:1)
- *Born of a Virgin* (Prophesied: Isaiah 7:14; Prophecy Fulfilled: Matthew 1:18-20)
- *Riding a Donkey* (Prophesied: Zechariah 9:9; Prophecy Fulfilled: Mark 11:1-10)
- *Cleansing of the Temple* (Prophesied: Psalm 69:9; Prophecy Fulfilled: John 2:13ff)
- *Messiah Despised* (Prophesied: Isaiah 53:3; Prophecy Fulfilled: John 8:48ff)
- *Messiah's Suffering* (Prophesied: Isaiah 53; Prophecy Fulfilled: Acts 13:13ff)

- *A Lamb to the Slaughter* (Prophesied: Isaiah 53:7-8; Prophecy Fulfilled: Acts 8:30-35)
- *Pierced Hands and Feet* (Prophesied: Psalm 22:16; Prophecy Fulfilled: John 19:18ff)
- *Not a Bone Broken* (Prophesied: Psalm 34:20; Prophecy Fulfilled: John 19:33)
- *Lots Cast for Clothes* (Prophesied: Psalm 22:18; Prophecy Fulfilled: Matthew 27:35)
- *Messiah Killed* (Prophesied: Isaiah 53; Prophecy Fulfilled: Acts 13:26ff)
- *Died with Transgressors* (Prophesied: Isaiah 53:12b; Prophecy Fulfilled: Mark 15:27-28)
- *Messiah Resurrected* (Prophesied: Isaiah 53; Prophecy Fulfilled: Acts 17:1-4)

I could list hundreds of other fulfilled prophecies about Christ, but these certainly show that what the Bible prophesied has indeed come to pass.

In his preaching, Paul argued from and with the authority of the prophetic words of Scripture:

> As his custom was, Paul went into the synagogue, and on three Sabbath days he reasoned with them from the Scriptures, explaining and proving that the Christ had to suffer and rise from the dead. "This Jesus I am proclaiming to you is the Christ," he said (Acts 17:2-3).

Paul also could say:

> For what I received I passed on to you as of first importance, that Christ died for our sins according to the Scriptures, that he was buried, that he was raised on the third day, according to the Scriptures (1 Corinthians 15:3-5a).

Verification through fulfilled prophecy is emphasized in many other passages in Scripture, such as Matthew 1:22-23, 2:23, 5:17-18; Luke 18:31-33; Acts 13:27-29; Romans 1:2-3; and Revelation 10:7.

3. Reliability of biblical documents.

Existing Old Testament texts from a millennium ago have been cross-examined with the Samaritan Pentateuch, the Septuagint (a third century B.C. Greek translation of the Old Testament), the Targum and Talmud (writings and commentaries related to the Hebrew Scriptures), and the relatively recently discovered Dead Sea Scrolls. The result? More confidence than ever that the Old Testament we have today is virtually identical with the original writings.

What about the New Testament? The quantity of manuscripts is one of the most overwhelming evidences of accuracy. We have more than 5,000 ancient Greek manuscripts, more than 8,000 ancient Latin manuscripts, plus about 1,000 more ancient manuscripts in other languages. No other writings from antiquity have anywhere near as much textual support pointing us accurately toward the original writings.

Furthermore, the entire Bible refers to events documented and described in secular history. One example of this is a secular reference to Jesus Christ in a letter written shortly after A.D. 73 by a prisoner named Mara Bar-Serapion. The letter compares the deaths of Pythagoras, Socrates, and Christ.

Other secular contemporaries of Christ mention Him: Tacitus, Suetonius, Pliny the Younger, and Lucian. The Jewish Talmud also mentions Jesus a number of times.

4. Its remarkable unity and coherence.

The Bible was written by a diversity of some forty authors over a period of more than 1,500 years. It includes narratives, letters, poetry, prophecies, sermons, and wisdom literature. The Bible is a compilation of sixty-six separate books, yet is unified in its message from cover to cover.

The Bible has one theme: redemption. From the opening pages of Genesis to the last pages of Revelation at the end of Scripture, this one theme is singular and constant.

5. Its ability to transform lives.

From the first generation on, Christians were accused of turning the world upside down (Acts 17:6). The power of the Gospel revealed in Scripture has changed tens of millions of people's lives for several thousand years.

The Bible is the only book that gives solid answers to life's ultimate questions. It fully answers the questions:

- Who am I?
- Where did I come from?
- Why am I here?
- Where am I going?
- What is the purpose of my existence?

Someone has put it this way:

This book contains the mind of God, the state of man, the way of salvation, the doom of sinners, the happiness of believers. Its doctrines are holy. Its precepts are binding. Its histories are true and its decisions are immutable. Read it to be wise, believe it to be safe, and practice it to be holy. It contains light to direct you, food to support you, and comfort to cheer you. It is the traveler's map, the pilgrim's staff, the pilot's compass, the soldier's sword, and the Christian's character. Christ is its grand subject, our good its design, and the glory of God its end. It should fill the memory, ruffle the heart, and guide the feet. Read it slowly, frequently, prayerfully. It is a mine of wealth, a paradise of glory, and a river of pleasure. It's given you in life, will be open at Judgment, and remembered forever.

It involves the highest responsibility, rewards the greatest labor, and condemns all who trifle with its holy contents.

Each of us must settle the question about whether the Bible is God's holy, authoritative, and infallible Word. If it is, then we must come to grips with the Bible's main message: that we must trust Jesus Christ alone for our salvation and live for Him.

Oh, yes, you might wonder whatever happened to Dirk. With his brilliant mind, Dirk began to examine the evidences that show that Scripture is indeed the Word of God. About a year after my first visit with him, he confessed his faith in Jesus Christ and gave his life to Him!

■ ■ ■ ■ ■

More biblical counsel

HEBREWS 4:12

I THESSALONIANS 2:13

ROMANS 15:4

2 TIMOTHY 3:16-17

ACTS 20:32

PSALM 1

PSALM 33:4

PSALM 119:74

PSALM 119:114

ISAIAH 40:8

MARK 13:31

Doubting One's Salvation

As for God, his way is perfect;
the word of the Lord is flawless.
He is a shield for all who take refuge in Him.

2 SAMUEL 22:31

■ ■ ■ ■ ■

Most of life is uncertain, unpredictable, in a state of constant flux and change. We can't count on job security anymore, let alone our health. The weather is totally unpredictable—ask any meteorologist! The stock market certainly fluctuates—up one day, down the next. Many marriages aren't sure. Is it any wonder Christians sometimes question the solidity and certainty of their eternal salvation?

Sue sang in our church choir. A single mom with two grade school age children, she had her share of struggles. But she always seemed up, with a lovely smile and her favorite expression, "Hey, God is in control, no sweat!" So I was somewhat taken back when Sue came to me one day and said, "I'm not even sure I'm saved."

Sue's story was sadly familiar. She accepted Jesus Christ when she was eleven years old, was active for Christ during high school, but fell away from the Lord when she went to the university. Parties, drinking, drugs, and even sex marked her life her freshman year.

Sue became pregnant at nineteen, married the father, and had one more child. Then her husband left her for another woman when their second baby was only three months old.

Jobless, saddled with two children, and newly divorced, Sue found herself in deep depression. When she had all but reached bottom, a friend called and invited her to our church. It was a turning point in her life.

Though Sue went through deep repentance and recommitted her life to Christ, she didn't feel accepted by the Lord. In her heart, she feared she had lost her salvation while living such a wild and undisciplined life her first year in college.

Some would say, "If you doubt your salvation, then you must not be saved, since the Bible says we can *know* we're saved." But wait a minute! Man doubts what he tends to believe. The presence of doubt presupposes the existence of a truth which can be doubted.

I believe that not only may a true Christian doubt his or her salvation, such doubt sometimes can be healthy—especially if it sends that person to God and His Word to make sure.

Dwight L. Moody used to say he never knew anyone who was effective in the service of Christ who did not first of all have complete assurance of his or her salvation. When a person lives in fear, wondering if he is saved, he certainly isn't in a position to minister to others in Jesus' name. Settle the big question first, then live for Christ all you please!

HOW CAN I KNOW I'M SAVED?

Before I proceed further, allow me to ask: How do you know you were saved in the first place? Have you come to God, taking the steps outlined in Scripture? Perhaps you've never seen a clear presentation of the gospel. The following steps answer the question, "What must I do to be saved?" (Acts 16:31).

1. Admit that you have sinned against God.

It's sometimes hard to acknowledge we're sinful, because naturally most people think they're "good." Compared to God's righteous standard, however, "all have sinned" (Romans 3:23). As part of the fallen human race, our natural tendency toward sin is inbred. Even King David admitted: "Surely I was sinful at birth, sinful from the time my mother conceived me" (Psalm 51:5).

2. Understand the consequences of your sin.

"So, nobody's perfect. What's the big deal?" The Bible tells us that sin has separated us from God (Isaiah 59:2). Scripture also teaches that sin produces spiritual death within us (Romans 6:23) and places us under a curse (Galatians 3:10). Because of our sin, we deserve God's judgment.

3. Realize that Jesus Christ is our only solution to sin.

Jesus said, "I am the way and the truth and the life. No one comes to the Father except through me" (John 14:6). Since He alone died to pay the penalty our sin incurred, He alone is able to save us.

4. Receive Christ as your Savior.

We must receive Him into our lives before we are saved. This is done by repenting of our sins (Acts 3:19), believing in Christ (Acts 16:31), then openly confessing Jesus as Lord (Romans 10:9-10). The Bible promises: "Everyone who calls on the name of the Lord will be saved" (Romans 10:13).

The good news is that you may call on the Lord *right now* before you finishing reading this page. If you're willing to do that, please, stop for a minute and pray a prayer something like this:

> *Lord Jesus, I acknowledge that I'm a sinner. I know I can't save myself. I now receive You into my life as Savior and Lord. I'm truly sorry for my sin, and I now accept Your love and full forgiveness. I look forward to living with You forever in heaven. Please bless my family. May they come to know You, too. Amen.*

If you truly believe in Jesus Christ, and receive His promise of eternal life and forgiveness of sins, you're instantly part of His forever family!

If that's your decision today, please write your name and the date in the spaces provided on the next page.

```
I have trusted Jesus Christ as my Savior.

_____
Signature

_____
Date
```

REASONS PEOPLE LOSE THEIR ASSURANCE

If it's clear from Scripture how to become a Christian, why do some people later doubt their salvation? In my counseling experience, I often come across the following seven reasons.

1. Some don't know what God's Word says.

The most famous doubter in the Bible is Thomas. After hearing that Jesus had appeared to the other apostles after rising from the dead, Thomas was incredulous. He said, "Unless I see the nail marks in his hands, and put my fingers where the nails were, and put my hand in his side, I will not believe" (John 20:25b).

Why wouldn't Thomas believe? For one thing, he had forgotten the prophecy Jesus had made earlier that He would be killed and on the third day would rise again. Had he remembered those words and believed, all doubt would have vanished.

I've talked to many people who have doubted their salvation in Christ. Most had never read the biblical reasons they can know for certain whether or not they are saved.

2. Some trust only in their senses and reason.

Notice again what Thomas said: "Unless I see.... Unless I touch." His philosophy of life was: "If I can see it, touch it, smell it, taste it, or hear it, then it's real. If I can't, it's not." Thomas had wrongly elevated his five senses above God's own Word.

Others make reason the highest ground of authority. Again, such an approach places anything beyond man's sensory perceptions and rational analysis outside the realm of what is knowable, let alone true.

Apologist Josh McDowell used to joke that doubting Thomas must have been a graduate student. Most secular higher learning today prompts skepticism and cynicism. Supposedly intelligent men and women reject anything in Scripture they can't understand. Thus Jesus Christ is dismissed out of hand, because His virgin birth, miracles, death on the cross for our sins, resurrection, and ascension are "beyond the scope of science and reason."

Beyond the scope of science? Yes, as is all of history! The scope of science is actually quite narrow, if you think about it. It can only deal with that which is reproducible and repeatable in a controlled setting. Science can no more prove you had breakfast yesterday morning than it can prove man first landed on the moon in 1969. Those are facts of history, not science!

Beyond the scope of reason? Yes, many facts are beyond our limited understanding. We all use electricity, but even many scientists don't fully understand it. We all watch television, but most of us have no idea how pictures are formed within the rather peculiar looking boxes sitting in our living rooms. When it comes to the things of God, then, upon what basis can anyone blatantly reject as unknowable or false what they don't yet understand?

3. Some rely too heavily on their feelings.

We live in a feelings-oriented society. "If it feels good, do it," is the motto of the day. It's no wonder, then, that many base the security of their salvation on their feelings. Some come to Christ on a wave of emotion, but when the warm fuzzies are gone, they conclude they must have lost their salvation, too.

A few days after I led one man to Christ, he called me on the phone. "I don't feel saved anymore," he told me. "After we prayed in your office, I sinned again." Obviously, the euphoria of his salvation evaporated at that point.

Since I knew this man fairly well, I immediately asked him if he were married. When he answered affirmatively, I asked if he always "felt" married. He paused for quite a while, seeing my point. I then asked him if he were an American citizen. "Yes," he replied. I then asked him if he always felt like an American on a daily basis. Of course not.

Contrary to popular rumor, reality isn't based on how we feel. Nowhere in the Bible are we told to look for warm fuzzy feelings to make certain we are saved.

Our eternal relationship with God cannot be based on feelings. Instead, we must base our salvation on the fact of the finished work of Christ on the cross and His empty tomb. If we know why we needed to be saved, and how we received salvation through faith, then we must continue to depend on what God's Word says, not on our feelings.

God says we can and should know we have the gift of eternal life abiding in us:

> I write these things to you who believe in the name of the Son of
> God, so that you may know that you have eternal life (1 John 5:13).

4. Some fall back into a sinful way of life.

Through the years, I've learned to ask people questioning their salvation whether or not they struggle with any reoccurring sin in their life. I've found in more cases than not, this is a major a source of doubt.

The psalmist David admitted:

> When I kept silent, my bones wasted away, through my groaning
> all day long...my strength was sapped as in the heat of summer
> (Psalm 32:3-4).

Disobedience in even a small area can rob a Christian of his or her assurance that "it is well with my soul." When we allow sin to dominate our lives, it becomes a wedge driving us further away from a close relationship with Jesus Christ.

Jesus told the story of the now infamous prodigal son. The Bible tells us that during his time away from his father, this young man went from bad to worse. Broke, sick, alone, ashamed, he finally came crawling back to his father, but only when "he came to his senses" (Luke 15:17).

Sin and disobedience pull us away from any security and sense of well-being we ever had. Worse, many try to cover their sin, gloss over it, or pretend that "it isn't so bad after all."

Scripture, however, warns: "He who conceals his sins does not prosper, but whoever confesses and renounces them finds mercy" (Proverbs 28:13).

5. Some don't know yet who they are in Christ.

Ignorance of our identity in Christ can lead to lack of assurance. Scripture teaches that, as Christians, we are:

Children of God	1 John 3:1
Righteous in God's eyes	2 Corinthians 5:21
Justified	Romans 5:1
Sanctified	1 Corinthians 6:11
Free from condemnation	Romans 8:1
Heirs with Christ	Romans 8:17
God's inheritance	Ephesians 1:18
More than conquerors	Romans 8:37
Redeemed	1 Peter 1:18
New creations	2 Corinthians 5:17

Our assurance of salvation is wrapped up in our identity. If Satan can convince us we're a bunch of "nobodies," he can steal our assurance of salvation.

6. Some think we must do good works to remain saved.

At least one theological school of thought today says we receive salvation solely by grace—God's free, unmerited, undeserved, unearned gift...but in order to keep saved, we supposedly must do certain good works to prove our profession of faith was genuine. This "performance mentality" theology robs many of any sense of assurance of salvation.

The Bible teaches we are not only brought into salvation by grace, but also remain saved and secure thanks to God's grace and might (1 Peter 1:3-5).

There is a place for good works, because we love the Lord. Good works confirm we are saved, but they certainly aren't the means to obtain or maintain our salvation (Ephesians 2:10).

7. Some haven't grown in their Christian life yet.

If over a period of months a baby fails to grow physically and mentally, we become alarmed. "Arrested development" is serious! Yet we think nothing of it if a Christian doesn't grow in the first year of his or her new relationship with the Lord.

Biblically, we're commanded to "grow in the grace and knowledge of our Lord and Savior, Jesus Christ" (2 Peter 3:18). Growth comes by getting into God's Word (Colossians 3:16), attending church (Hebrews 10:24-25), prayer (Ephesians 6:18), telling others about Christ (Acts 1:8), and by serving the Lord through ministry to other people (1 Peter 4:10).

Whatever the cause of your doubts about your salvation, let's turn to God's Word to address this problem head-on and settle the issue once and for all.

COUNSEL FROM GOD'S WORD

Before we see from Scripture how you can make sure of your salvation, let's consider how God Himself has made sure of your salvation.

HOW HAS GOD MADE SURE OF MY SALVATION?

I. By His love.

God's everlasting love toward you confirms the fact that you cannot lose your salvation. The apostle Paul writes:

> Since we have now been justified by his blood how much more
> shall we be saved from God's wrath through him! For if, when we
> were God's enemies, we were reconciled to him through the death
> of his Son, how much more, having been reconciled, shall we be
> saved through his life!(Romans 5:9-10).

This is often called the argument from the greater to the lesser. In other words, if God's love had no problem saving us when we were sinful and rebellious, is He really going to have any problem keeping us saved? The answer is obvious: No!

Later in that same epistle Paul affirms:

> For I am convinced that neither death nor life, neither angels nor
> demons, neither the present nor the future, nor any powers, neither
> height nor depth, nor anything else in all creation, will be able to sepa-

rate us from the love of God that is in Christ Jesus (Romans 8:38-39).

2. By His "seed" in us.

The Bible says when we are saved, we enter a very unique relationship with God—we become His child. We're all children of God if we've believe in Christ (Galatians 3:26).

Our first birth is the result of the seed of our earthly parents. When your father's sperm fertilized your mother's egg, you were created! The only problem is, we were born of perishable seed, destined to one day die.

But when you and I are born "again," God's seed is permanently planted in our heart:

> For you have been born again, not of perishable seed, but of imperishable, through the living and enduring word of God (1 Peter 1:23).

That means the new life God formed in us when we are saved is permanent. It will never end. Just as you can't "un-child" yourself biologically, no one can spiritually "un-child" us from God. We are part of His forever family!

3. By His seal on us.

The Bible teaches that when you are saved, you are "sealed" with the Holy Spirit:

> Having believed, you were marked in Him with a seal, the promised Holy Spirit, who is a deposit guaranteeing our inheritance until the redemption of those who are God's possession—to the praise of his glory (Ephesians 1:13b-14).

The word "seal" means mark. It's an indelible mark. If we can lose our salvation, then God's seal—the Holy Spirit—is defective, which is impossible. The fact that He permanently indwells us confirms our inheritance is guaranteed (2 Corinthians 1:22, 5:5).

4. By His redemption.

Scripture speaks of our "eternal redemption" (Hebrews 9:12). The term "to redeem" means to buy back. Jesus purchased us at the price of His own blood:

> For you know it was not with perishable things such as silver and gold that you were redeemed from the empty way of life handed down to you from your forefathers, but with the precious blood of Christ, a lamb without blemish or defect (1 Peter 1:18).

If we could lose our salvation, it would mean Satan must have come up with a greater price than Jesus paid, which is ludicrous. Jesus paid the ultimate price—His own blood. There is no higher price! If you are saved, it's confirmed forever by the blood of Christ.

5. By the prayers of Jesus.

Since God hears and answers the prayers of His one and only Son, and since Jesus prays for our salvation on a continual basis, we absolutely cannot lose our salvation:

> Therefore he is able to save completely those who come to God through him, because he always lives to intercede for them (Hebrews 7:25).

Also, we're told in 1 John 2:1 that if we sin as Christians, "we have one who speaks to the Father in our defense." This means that long before we will ever stand before God, Jesus is going to our defense. His successful appeals to the Father—on the basis of His atoning sacrifice for our sins on the cross—confirm the security and assurance of our salvation.

6. By the promises of Jesus.

Jesus Himself has given us rock-solid promises of the assurance of our salvation:

> "All that the Father gives me will come to me, and whoever comes to me I will never drive away. For I have come from heaven not to do my will but to do the will of him who sent me. And

this is the will of him who sent me, that I shall lose none of all that he has given me, but raise them up at the last day" (John 6:37-39).

Furthermore, Jesus made a promise that once we are in His hands, we cannot be removed:

"My sheep listen to my voice; I know them, and they follow me. I give them eternal life and they shall never perish; no one can snatch them out of my hand" (John 10:27-28).

"No one" means absolutely no one. It means Satan can't, your enemies can't, circumstances can't, and you can't. Your salvation is guaranteed!

7. By His faithfulness and commitment to us.

The Lord has committed Himself to our salvation:

"Can a mother forget the baby at her breast and have no compassion on the child she has borne? Though she may forget, I will not forget you! See, I have engraved you on the palms of my hands; your walls are ever before me" (Isaiah 49:15-16).

Again, the Lord has promised to keep us strong to the end:

He will keep you strong to the end, so that you will be blameless on the day of our Lord Jesus Christ. God, who has called you into fellowship with his Son Jesus Christ our Lord, is faithful (1 Corinthians 1:8-9).

If we could lose our salvation, then the faithfulness of God and His integrity would be called into serious question. God will not go back on His Word. What God begins, He completes:

. . .being confident of this, that he who began good work in you will carry it on to completion until the day of Christ Jesus (Philippians 1:6).

Again, Paul reminded the Thessalonians of the faithfulness of God in keeping us blameless to the end:

> May God himself, the God of peace, sanctify you through and
> through. May your whole spirit, soul, and body be kept blameless
> at the coming of our Lord Jesus Christ. The one who calls you is
> faithful and he will do it (1 Thessalonians 5:23-24).

Many other passages listed below also bear witness to God's faithfulness to complete the salvation He began in us. The Lord certainly has done everything He can to guarantee our salvation.

HOW CAN I BE SURE OF MY SALVATION?

1. By accepting the promises of God as true.

The Bible says: "Believe in the Lord Jesus, and you will be saved" (Acts 16:31). In that short verse, we have both a command and a promise. The command is clear: "Believe in the Lord Jesus." That means put your full trust and confidence in Him, and Him alone, as the only source and provider of your salvation. If you do that, the promise is clear: "you will be saved."

If I invite you over to my house Tuesday evening at seven o'clock for a delicious steak dinner, when you come you expect to be fed a steak dinner. Whether you will or won't depends on the power of my word and its reliability.

Jesus said: "I tell you the truth, whoever hears my word and believes him who sent me has eternal life and will not be condemned; he has crossed over from death to life" (John 5:24). His word is reliable and true, powerful and unchanging. This one promise alone is enough to assure us we can't lose our salvation.

2. By understanding God wants us to know we're saved.

Perhaps the most famous verse on the assurance of salvation is found toward the end of the Bible:

> I write these things to you who believe in the name of the Son of
> God that you may know that you have eternal life (1 John 5:13).

If we believe in Jesus, we can know beyond any shadow of a doubt that we have eternal life. God meant for us to know for sure. Christianity is a "know-so" faith. It's not, "I think so, or I hope so, or I guess so," but "I know so!"

Paul could affirm:

I know whom I have believed and am convinced that he is able to guard what I have entrusted to him for that day (2 Timothy 1:12b).

You don't have to go through this life "hoping" you are saved, but always waiting till you die to find out for sure. You can know for sure, today!

3. By passing the "bearing fruit" test.

How will we know if someone is a Christian? How will we know if we ourselves are saved? Jesus said to look for "fruit" that is, a godly life overflowing with good character and good deeds done for others in Jesus' name.

Jesus told His disciples how to recognize other disciples:

"By their fruit you will recognize them....Likewise every good tree bears good fruit, but a bad tree bears bad fruit. A good tree cannot bear bad fruit, and a bad tree cannot bear good fruit.... Thus, by their fruit you will recognize them" (Matthew 7:16-20).

Those are strong words. Is Jesus saying that a person isn't a Christian if he doesn't always bear good fruit? No, not at all. But if a person really knows the Lord, there will be some good fruit in his life.

In fact, Jesus went on to say:

"This is to my Father's glory, that you bear much fruit, showing yourselves to be my disciples" (John 15:8).

One proof that we are Christ's disciples is the amount of good fruit we bear in our lives. If you are a Christian, and the Holy Spirit is producing fruit in your life (Galatians 5:22-23), banish any doubts you may have about the assurance of your salvation.

4. By sensing the witness of the Holy Spirit in your life.

The Bible says that when we are born again, God gives us the Holy Spirit. He actually takes up residence in our life, and we become the "temple" where He resides:

Don't you know that you yourselves are God's temple and that God's Spirit lives in you? (1 Corinthians 3:16).

As soon as He indwells us, the Holy Spirit imparts spiritual gifts to us (1 Corinthians 12:7-11), strengthens our prayers (Romans 8:26), leads us into all truth (John 14:26, 16:13), and makes us victorious over the flesh (Galatians 5:16).

Perhaps the greatest ministry the Holy Spirit has in our lives is confirming and bearing witness with our human spirits that we really are children of God. Paul writes, "The Spirit himself testifies with our spirit that we are God's children" (Romans 8:16).

While in some cases God's Spirit may do His confirming work independent of the Word of God, He usually uses what is already promised to confirm in our hearts that we are children of God, and thus heirs to His glorious riches.

5. By continuing to believe in Jesus Christ.

If you are doubting whether or not you're still saved, even though you trusted Jesus Christ for your salvation sometime in the past, ask yourself this question: "Do I still believe in Jesus Christ as my Savior, Lord, and Messiah?"

Jesus made it clear that if we truly have the gift of eternal life and salvation, it will be an ongoing belief (John 5:24). The apostle John made the same exact point: "Everyone who believes that Jesus is the Christ is born of God" (1 John 5:1). In the original language the New Testament was written in, the verb "believe" is in the present, active tense in that verse and in John 5:24. Scripture is speaking of an ongoing belief, one that never ends.

6. By obeying the commands of Jesus.

Do you have the assurance of salvation? Ask yourself one last question: "Am I doing what Jesus said?" The apostle John writes:

We know that we have come to know him if we obey his commands. The man who says, "I know him," but does not do what he commands is a liar, and the truth is not in him. But if anyone obeys his word, God's love is truly made complete in him. This is how we know we are in him: Whoever claims to live in him must walk as Jesus did (1 John 2:3-5).

This does *not* mean you'll lose your salvation if you disobey one of the Lord's commands. Just the opposite! The key word is "keep." The word literally means to "navigate by the stars."

John is urging us to "navigate by Jesus' commandments." Just as a ship that steered by the stars in ancient days didn't always stay on course, so we don't always stay on course. We lose our way sometimes. We fail to obey. What happens then? Thank God, the blood of Jesus cleanses us "from all sin" (1 John 1:7).

If we are Christians, the basic pattern of our lives will be obedience to Jesus, even though we may get off course at times. When we disobey, we are grieved. Great Bible heroes such as Peter and King David were severely grieved when they sinned against God (Psalm 51:1-4, Matthew 26:75).

Part of obeying Jesus is loving our brothers and sisters in Christ: "We know that we have passed from death to life, because we love our brothers" (1 John 3:14).

If you have a permanent hatred in your heart against another Christian, and you have no intention of ever making that right, then you do have reason to question your salvation.

One proof that you are saved is an eventual desire to harbor no ill-will against other members of your spiritual family.

What about Sue?

Once she learned that it wasn't her good works that got her into salvation, and it wasn't her good life or works that kept her saved, but that God's grace was responsible on both accounts, she gained a tremendous assurance of salvation.

Sue also learned the value of 1 John 1:7, cited above, which says that we are constantly being cleansed from sin by the blood of Christ. What a wonderful promise, indeed!

More biblical counsel

JOB 19:25-27

1 JOHN 4:13-16

2 TIMOTHY 2:12-13

2 CORINTHIANS 5:17

1 JOHN 1:7-9

JOHN 1:12

EPHESIANS 2:8-9

ROMANS 11:29

ROMANS 8:28-30

HEBREWS 10:14

2 TIMOTHY 4:18

TITUS 3:4-5

JUDE 24

REVELATION 3:5

1 JOHN 3:19-20

HEBREWS 11:6

PSALM 119:89-90

2 PETER 1:19

1 JOHN 1:7-9

PSALM 42:5-6

PSALM 16:5-6

Envy

*Love is patient, love is
kind. It does not envy...*
1 CORINTHIANS 13:4

■ ■ ■ ■

Katie and Brenda met during their senior year in high school and became the best of friends. They were practically inseparable. But then the boy Brenda had been dating off and on asked Katie to the school dance. Soon thereafter, Katie was selected over several other girls—including Brenda—for the leading role in the upcoming school play. It was more than Brenda could take. She "blew a fuse," destroying her friendship with Katie.

What happened to Brenda in a "weak" moment happens to all of us when we allow the spirit of envy to color our thinking about others.

Envy is coveting what someone is or has, and feeling bitter and angry because you feel you deserve the same or better. It's a killer attitude.

Solomon put it this way: "A heart of peace gives life to the body, but envy rots the bones" (Proverbs 14:30). Envy is like leukemia of the heart, destroying our ability to think or reason. As a result, we end up lashing out at others without just cause.

Since envy obviously isn't one of the fruits of the Spirit, it's essential that we answer the question, "What produces envy within us?"

1. A distorted view of ourselves.

God made each of us different. We all have distinct temperaments, talents, time commitments, financial resources, and family backgrounds. You're not like me. I'm not like you. We all come in different shapes, sizes, and colors.

Yet individual differences sparked the first case of envy recorded in the Bible. At the heart of the matter was Cain's distorted view of himself. Both Cain and his brother, Abel, brought an offering to the Lord. God looked with favor on Abel's offering, but not on Cain's. Cain's face became "downcast" (Genesis 4:5).

On the inside, Cain was seething with envy. Notice, the Bible doesn't say God was displeased with Cain, only with his offering. But Cain took it personally, became extremely jealous of Abel, took him out into a field, and murdered him.

What else causes envy?

2. A false perception of what we need.

Brenda felt Katie had somehow taken everything that was important to her. Brenda didn't *need* the attention of a certain boy or the lead role in the school play to be a whole person, but in her mind, she felt she did.

3. Lack of faith in the sovereignty of God.

When a person becomes highly envious of what another has or is, it is tantamount to saying, "Here is an area where God obviously is not in control." While a Christian would never say such a thing out loud, we certainly *feel* that way when we begin to envy someone else.

A man I knew and a co-worker of his once entered a contest. The co-worker won a free trip to Hawaii. The man I knew became extremely envious of the other man. He even went as far as to say, "and the Lord knew that I was the one who needed that vacation, not Frank!"

4. Self-centeredness.

Envy always reveals a self-centered, me-first attitude of the heart. Instead of rejoicing with those who rejoice, bitterness emerges. Brenda wanted the attention of a certain boy because it would puff up her ego and sense of self-esteem. She wanted the lead role in the school play because it would make her look sharp and talented in the eyes of her peers. She certainly wasn't looking out for the interests of others.

5. Insecurity.

I've noticed that insecure people tend to become envious of others, mistakenly thinking if they had what others have, they would be more secure.

The psalmist said it well: "I was young, and now I am old, yet I have never seen the righteous forsaken or their children begging bread" (Psalm 37:25).

God is faithful and will give us all we need. Our security doesn't rest on *what* we have materially or *who* we are, but on *Whose* we are. We are God's children. He loves us and will provide everything we need. Peter says it well: "His divine power has given us everything we need for life and godliness" (2 Peter 1:3). "Everything" means everything. If He doesn't give it, we don't need it. In poverty and in wealth, we need to trust in Him, not things.

6. Unbridled anger.

When someone has done something to make us angry, it's amazing how often our tendency is also to become envious of that person. The more anger we feel toward that him or her, the more envious we often become.

Whatever our reason for feeling envious, we must deal with it biblically.

COUNSEL FROM GOD'S WORD

I suggest you take these steps in order to gain freedom from envy today.

1. Confess your envy as a sin against God and ask for His forgiveness.

Envy isn't a personality quirk; the Bible calls it a sin. It ranks right up there with hatred and drunkenness in the apostle Paul's list of the deeds of the sinful nature (Galatians 5:21). All such sin needs to be confessed to God (1 John 1:9). Then ask and thank God for His forgiveness.

2. Confess your envy to the person you've offended.

The Bible says, "Therefore, confess your sins to each other, and pray for each other" (James 5:16). What better person to confess the sin of envy to than the person whom you have sinned against? You might want to say something like this: "I know I've acted envious of you, and now realize that was wrong. Will you forgive me?"

3. Resolve to be content with what you are and have.

When you get into God's Word, it's amazing how much importance He places on being content with our lot in life.

Paul reminds us of a very important truth:

> But godliness with contentment is great gain. For we brought nothing into the world, and we can take nothing out of it.
> But if we have food and clothing, we will be content with that
> (1 Timothy 6:6-8).

He could also say, "I have learned to be content whatever the circumstances" (Philippians 4:11). From whom did Paul learn that secret? None other than the Lord Himself.

Jesus gave a stern warning in the material possessions department when He said:

> "Watch out! Be on your guard against all kinds of greed; a
> man's life does not consist in the abundance of his possessions" (Luke 12:15).

Since greed and envy are first cousins, we could easily insert the word "envy" where greed appears in that warning!

The Bible also says concerning our material possessions:

Keep your lives free from the love of money and be content with what you have, because God has said, "Never will I leave you; never will I forsake you" (Hebrews 13:5).

We need to be willing to say with the psalmist:

Lord, you have assigned me my portion and my cup; you have made my lot secure. The boundary lines have fallen for me in pleasant places; surely I have a delightful heritage (Psalm 16:5-6).

4. Ask yourself the $64,000 question.

And what is that question? Namely, "Do I have really a right to have what that other person has?"

To honestly answer that question, ruthlessly ask yourself: "Is this something I need, or merely something I want? Will God truly be glorified if I have it? Will it really make me a better witness for Christ?"

5. Remember whose responsibility others are.

Sometimes it's easy to envy what other people are or what they have if you "know" they don't deserve that house, that car, that title, that position of honor.

Let me remind you that such concerns are God's department, not yours. If you're fighting the sin of envy, replace it with trust—trust in a God who truly is in control of your life *and* the life of that other person.

Remember Brenda? You'll be glad to know she learned a shocking but valuable lesson when Katie told her their "dream" boy had been arrested for attempted rape of another girl. "Just to think," Brenda confided, "I was coveting and envious for the very person who could have ruined my life."

How often the very thing we think we need is the very thing that could bring about our destruction. Thankfully, Brenda and Katie's friendship was restored, unfortunately through a hard lesson.

·····

More biblical counsel

PROVERBS 6:34

PROVERBS 23:17

ECCLESIASTES 4:4

ECCLESIASTES 9:5-6

PSALM 37:1

PSALM 73:3

PROVERBS 27:4

PROVERBS 24:1,19

JOB 5:2

PROVERBS 3:31

ROMANS 1:29

1 CORINTHIANS 3:1-3

JAMES 3:13-14

2 CORINTHIANS 12:20

Fear

The Lord is my light and my salvation—
whom shall I fear?

PSALM 27:1

■ ■ ■ ■ ■

At the end of a long day, one mom requested of her rather timid son, "Billy, please go to the back porch and bring me the broom." "Oh, no, Mom, I can't," Billy protested. "The porch is dark, and I'm terribly afraid!"

"You needn't be afraid," his mother replied. "The Lord is out there."

Billy went to the edge of the porch, quickly looked up, and said, "Lord, hand me the broom!"

Well, you have to hand it to Billy. If God is big enough to be in a scary place, He's big enough to hand him the broom.

Fear is real, even if the object of someone's fear isn't. Take Harvey, for instance. Handsome, in his early thirties, confident, Harvey was a chef in one of our city's leading restaurants and on his way to becoming an executive chef. He was married, with two small children.

Little by little, Harvey began to fear almost everything. He feared losing his good job, feared getting sick, feared driving his car in rush hour traffic, feared food poisoning. He even feared making love with his wife, saying, "I just know something is going to go wrong." Eventually, he put double bolts on all his doors and bought a guard dog.

Fear became the dominating factor in Harvey's life and began to affect his job, his marriage, and his life. He was extremely close to a mental breakdown when he finally came in for biblical counseling.

Fear is as old as the first human family. When Adam and Eve suddenly fell from their privileged position of innocence, fear gripped them:

> Then the man and his wife heard the sound of the Lord God as he was
> walking in the garden in the cool of the day, and they hid from the
> Lord God among the trees of the garden. But the Lord God called to
> the man, "Where are you?" He answered, "I heard you in the garden,
> and I was afraid, because I was naked; so I hid" (Genesis 3:8-10).

Certainly in this case, fear was the result of sin and disobedience. There are other causes of fear as well.

IS THERE A "GOOD" FEAR?

Not all fear is harmful, crippling, or destructive. Some fear is healthy and necessary! We are admonished time and time again in God's Word to "fear the Lord."

King Solomon wrote more than three thousand years ago: "The fear of the Lord is the beginning of knowledge" (Proverbs 1:7). And, "The fear of the Lord adds length to life but the years of the wicked are cut short" (Proverbs 10:27).

In describing a wife, another writer of Proverbs put it this way: "Charm is deceptive, and beauty is fleeting; but a woman who fears the Lord is to be praised" (Proverbs 31:30).

Jesus also taught that unsaved people should fear meeting their Maker:

> "Do not be afraid of those who kill the body but cannot kill the
> soul. Rather be afraid of the One who can destroy both soul and
> body in hell" (Matthew 10:28).

Furthermore, the Lord has given us all a sense of caution that helps protect us. Children learn to fear poisonous snakes and wild animals. They also develop a healthy fear of fire and water.

A smart electrician quickly develops a healthy fear of electricity. A good chemist has a deep respect for the chemicals with which he works. The wrong combination can blow him out of his laboratory for good!

HARMFUL FEARS

Some dictionaries describe scores of harmful fears. There is acrophobia (fear of high places), agoraphobia (fear of open spaces), claustrophobia (fear of small places), bathophobia (fear of deep places), haptephobia (fear of being touched), taphephobia (fear of being buried alive), and zoophobia (fear of animals). The list of phobias is practically endless!

I once read about a man who feared that people were constantly talking about him. He even had to stop going to football games, because every time a team huddled, he thought they were whispering about him!

President Roosevelt was right when he said, "The only thing we have to fear is fear itself."

The root cause of all harmful fear is a lack of faith in the sovereign Lord of the universe. The Bible teaches that God is in control of all of life. What He purposes, He does (Isaiah 46:11). Everything that happens to us is either God-caused or God-allowed. He either directly sends circumstances our way, or sovereignly allows them as part of His purpose. Nothing happens outside His sovereign control. If that's true, we really have nothing to fear.

Jesus taught His disciples this when a storm arose on the Sea of Galilee. Jesus came walking on the water in the midst of the storm as the disciples were struggling at the oars of their boat. His words to them are His words to us today: "Take courage! It is I. Don't be afraid" (Mark 6:50b).

The presence of Jesus means the absence of fear. Someone once gave me a desk motto: "Fear knocked; faith answered the door; no one was there!"

Another source of fear is concern that we don't measure up to others or their expectations. Again, we must remember that we are called to please God, not man. Even the apostle Paul said, "We are not trying to please men, but God who tests our hearts" (1 Thessalonians 2:4b).

So, what should you do if you're suffering from fear?

COUNSEL FROM GOD'S WORD

Here's a verse of Scripture worth memorizing and meditating upon, then applying to your situation today:

> For God did not give us a spirit of timidity [or fear, as some translations put it], but a spirit of power, of love, and of self-discipline (2 Timothy 1:7).

1. Acknowledge that harmful fear is not of God.

The key verse quoted above is clear: God is not the author of fear. Satan brings fear into our lives to try to get us to distrust the sovereign Lord. King David could write: "Even though I walk through the valley of the shadow of death, I will fear no evil" (Psalm 23:4).

2. Check the source of your fear. Ask yourself if it's bigger than God.

I have a sign in my office that reads, "God is greater than any problem I have." Whether it's debt, disease, family problems, or whatever, God is greater than any problem you and I will ever face.

3. Trust in God to banish your fear.

The words of God to Abraham—"Do not be afraid, for I am with you" (Genesis 26:24)—say it all. The presence of God means the absence of fear.

One of my very favorite verses to share with people is this:

> When I am afraid, I will trust in you (Psalm 56:3).

God spoke to Isaiah these comforting, faith-building words:

> "Fear not, for I have redeemed you; I have summoned you by name, you are mine. When you pass through the waters, I will be with you" (Isaiah 43:1b-2a).

4. Confess all known sin to God and claim His forgiveness.

A man once told his pastor he couldn't sleep at night because of fear. The pastor discovered that this man had committed a horrible sin after becoming a Christian and had never confessed it. Finally, at wit's end, he confessed the sin to God and his pastor, and has slept like a baby ever since.

5. Claim what God has actually given you.

In 2 Timothy 1:7, we're told that God has given us "a spirit of power, of love, and of self-discipline."

First, we have God's *power* in us, all we need to overcome any challenge Satan throws our way. The apostle Peter reminds us that God's "divine power has given us everything we need for life and godliness" (2 Peter 1:3). His power in us wards off fear. But we must claim it.

Second, we have been given a spirit of *love* for God and others. The apostle John tells us:

There is no fear in love. But perfect love drives out fear,
because fear has to do with punishment. The one who fears is
not made perfect in love (1 John 4:18).

Humanly speaking, we're not capable of perfect love. But because God's perfect love abides in us, we can get the upper hand on fear.

Third, Paul says we've been given a spirit of *self-discipline* or a "sound mind," as some translations put it.

Much of what we fear is not based on reality, but on supposition. I've heard Zig Ziglar say in his motivational messages that F-E-A-R is False Evidence that Appears Real. The spirit of self-discipline enables us to objectively counter Satan's often not-so-subtle attempts to provoke fear in us.

6. Take authority and rebuke the spirit of fear.

First, acknowledge that it doesn't belong in your life. Second, command Satan to stop bringing fear on your life.

If he can paralyze you with fear, he can render you ineffective for God's kingdom. You might want to command him in these words:

*Satan, I command you to stop bringing fear into my life. By the
blood of Christ and His resurrection, I denounce your ability to
inflict me with fear. You have no place in my life, so I command
you to leave, and in Jesus' name I break the bondage of fear right
now.*

Some people fear their home will be broken into, or their house will
catch fire, or they will be sexually assaulted, or someone will steal their
car.

Maybe you have been plagued with fears about losing your job, or
not having enough to retire on, or coming down with cancer or some
other dread disease.

Unfounded, Satan-inspired fear can do horrible things to us. The
Lord never intended for you live in a state of fear. Remember, you and
God always make a majority!

So many times, the thing we fear the most isn't true at all. The story
is told of a group of shipwrecked sailors drifting on the ocean in a small
life raft. After a couple of days lost at sea, surrounded by water, they were
literally dying of thirst.

Finally, just as all hope seemed lost, the shipwrecked sailors met
another small boat and one of the men on that boat yelled, "Let down your
buckets for a drink!" The advice felt like a cruel slap in the face, for every
sailor knows that drinking salt water only hastens one's demise.

But when the advice was repeated several times, one of the shipwrecked sailors dipped a bucket into the ocean and took a small drink. To
their utter astonishment, they discovered they had been drifting the whole
time in fresh water! It turns out they had been shipwrecked near the estu-
ary of the Amazon, which pumps a huge supply of fresh water out to sea
for many miles.

Like those sailors adrift at sea, many times our fears are baseless. We
simply need to let our buckets down and draw renewed strength from the
Lord. His Spirit is an ever-flowing stream of living water within us (John
7:37-39).

What about Harvey? I'm glad to say he was delivered from his multitude of fears when he finally grasped two important truths. The first discovery was that a pattern of fear had been woven into Harvey's life during early childhood. After his father abandoned Harvey, his two sisters, and his mother, they lived in a constant state of fear for several years. Part of what Harvey was experiencing as an adult was a carry-over from that period of childhood trauma, which Satan was using to destroy Harvey.

In addition, after studying God's Word, Harvey came to understand nothing in this life is too big for God to handle. One Scripture passage in particular helped him overcome his fears:

> You will not fear the terror of night, nor the arrow that flies by day, nor the pestilence that stalks in darkness, nor the plague that destroys at midday.... If you make the Most High your dwelling—even the Lord, who is my refuge—then no harm will befall you, no disaster will come near your tent (Psalm 91:5-6, 9-10).

I urge you to take God at His Word and, like Harvey, overcome your worst fears today.

■ ■ ■ ■ ■

More biblical counsel

ISAIAH 41:10

PSALM 37:25

JEREMIAH 1:8

ISAIAH 43:1-2

PSALM 34:4

ROMANS 8:15-16

PROVERBS 1:33

HEBREWS 13:5-6

PROVERBS 10:27

Financial Bondage

*The rich rule over
the poor and the borrower
is servant to the lender.*

PROVERBS 22:7

■ ■ ■ ■ ■

One of America's most popular theme songs goes like this: "I owe, I owe, so off to work I go!"

Not only has consumer debt in America reached an all-time high, but the inability to pay it off also has reached a record high. Bankruptcies used to be rare and were generally confined to business failures. Today many individuals, couples, and families are filing for bankruptcy.

Jerry was unusually somber when he entered my office and sat down. Tall, handsome, and personable, I would have never dreamed what he was about to spill.

At age twenty-six, Jerry's new sports car had just been repossessed. In his hand, he was holding court papers that called for 25 percent of his wages to be docked. On top of that, he had just received a notice evicting him from the apartment he was renting. In three days, he had to be out. He had no where to go and no way to get there, anyway. He was homeless, helpless, and hapless.

Jerry's face was ashen and drawn as he disclosed what had happened. It all started when he deferred his student loans, which amounted to more than $10,000. He couldn't even pay the interest anymore.

Furthermore, because he couldn't get a good job his first three years out of college, Jerry had used credit cards for almost all his out-of-pocket expenses —whether for food, fuel, clothes, or the latest in entertainment.

On top of that, Jerry had made the mistake of purchasing a new sports car on credit. His total debt exceeded $33,000!

He admitted, "I feel like I've received the sentence of death." He couldn't even begin to provide for his wife and child. They would be homeless in less than seventy-two hours.

Why do people end up in such terrible financial bondage? Here are the most common reasons:

1. The demand for instant gratification.

"I want what I want and I want it now!" Delayed gratification is all but unheard of these days. Only a generation ago, if someone wanted a new washing machine, but didn't have the money, by and large they waited until they could save up the money and then buy it. Today's motto is: "If you want it now, get it now, and pay for it later."

2. Irresponsible spending.

Though millions have been financially thrashed, most Americans still do not use a budget to plan their expenditures. The result? People end up buying things they want but don't really need. That accounts for nearly 35 percent of all consumer debt today.

3. Preoccupation with what's new.

Some people wouldn't dream of buying second-hand items, even though they could realize savings of up to 90 percent on many major purchases.

One woman recently mentioned buying a beautiful, stylish outfit at a consignment shop for $20. She said it had hardly been worn and showed absolutely no signs of wear. No one could tell she had bought it used. Because of the unique design, material, and buttons, the outfit was obviously quite expensive. Later, she saw a similar outfit priced at $135—on sale!

Cars, trucks, motorcycles, bicycles, lawn mowers, washers, dryers, refrigerators, and other big-ticket items cost drastically more when purchased new.

You lose $1,000 just driving a new car off the lot. Most Americans can realize substantial savings each year by shopping for quality used products, instead of insisting that everything they purchase be new.

4. Abuse of credit cards.

Perhaps the biggest bane on the people of America was the introduction of the credit card. By it, millions of Americans, without discipline, plunged themselves into consumer debt they could not pay. Debt in and of itself is not wrong biblically, but it is wrong to pile up debt we cannot pay.

Before we go one dollar further into debt, we need to remind ourselves what God's Word says: "The rich rule over the poor, and the borrower is servant to the lender" (Proverbs 22:7). How true that is. Anytime we borrow money, we place ourselves at the mercy of the lender, and in a sense are in bondage to them.

5. Failure to tithe one's income.

I have never counseled anyone in financial bondage who told me they were tithing. On the contrary, most tell me they have given virtually nothing to the cause of Christ. We cannot violate God's proven, unchanging financial principles, however, and expect to prosper and be blessed by God.

COUNSEL FROM GOD'S WORD

If you are deep in debt or some other type of financial bondage, the best way to emerge victoriously is to know and act upon these unswerving biblical principles.

1. Recognize that God owns everything; we are called to be good managers of what He's given to us.

That is principle number one, because it affects every other principle. The Bible makes it clear: "The earth is the Lord's, and everything in it, the world and all who live in it" (Psalm 24:1). The Lord Himself says, "the world is mine, and all that is in it" (Psalm 50:12b).

It's little wonder that King David said "everything" comes from the Lord (1 Chronicles 29:14). We own nothing. Instead, we are called to be managers, caretakers, stewards of what really belongs to God. The Lord releases resources to each person "according to his ability" (Matthew 25:15).

Someone may object, "But I worked hard to earn enough money to get what I've got. Nobody handed anything to me on a silver platter. It's all mine." Have you forgotten what God's Word says about your income?

> But remember the Lord, your God, for it is he who gives you the ability to produce wealth (Deuteronomy 8:18).

Because everything ultimately is the Lord's, we need to acknowledge that and treat all our possessions as a trust from Him.

2. Remember you're accountable to God.

Jesus stressed this principle in many of His parables. In the parable of the "talents" (a unit of money used in biblical times), Jesus makes it clear that having entrusting each of us with a certain amount of wealth, God will someday demand an accounting (Matthew 25:14-30).

In the parable of the tenants, Jesus goes on to say that God expects a return on His investment in us (Mark 12:1-12). The question will be, did we gladly acknowledge His Lordship? If not, how great our loss will be!

In the parable of the shrewd manager, Jesus says that in the end, God will judge our hearts and determine if we worshiped money or the Master.

Paul says the same thing: "Now it is required that those who have been given a trust must prove faithful" (1 Corinthians 4:2).

We are accountable to God for how we manage what He releases into our hands. He's concerned with how generously we give, and how wisely we spend the rest.

3. Realize that commitment follows our giving.

Jesus said, "For where your treasure is, there will your heart be also" (Matthew 6:21). This verse is often wrongly turned around to say that where our commitment is, there will our treasure be. No, Jesus said it the other way around! Whatever we heavily invest in produces a heartfelt commitment within us. People who give little or no tithe to their local church usually aren't actively involved in that church's ongoing ministries, either.

4. Develop a godly focus.

Most people who find themselves in financial bondage have misplaced priorities. The Bible is clear as to where our focus is to be. Jesus said it Himself:

"But seek first his kingdom and his righteousness, and all these things will be yours as well" (Matthew 6:33).

Our focus needs to be on God's kingdom, on spiritual things. This is not to say we're to shirk making a living. But the Bible teaches us that when making money is our number on objective, our life is out of line with God's will.

The apostle Paul warns:

For the love of money is a root of all kinds of evil. Some people, eager for money, have wandered from the faith, and pierced themselves with many griefs (1 Timothy 6:10).

Scripture commands us not to "seek" wealth. While it certainly isn't wrong to be rich, it is wrong to desire great wealth.

5. Apply the principle of the returned harvest.

Few have grasped this biblical principle: Whatever we give to the cause of Christ always comes back in abundance so we can give again.

It's like giving up a little water to prime a pump so we can have an abundant supply of water. Similarly, releasing funds back to the Lord brings back to us abundant funds, making it possible for us to release even more.

Jesus put it this way:

"Give and it will be given to you. A good measure, pressed down, shaken together, and running over, will be poured into your lap. For with the measure you use, it will be measured to you" (Luke 6:38).

Paul talks about the very same thing in 2 Corinthians 8-9. The Lord promises:

> "Bring the whole tithe into the storehouse, that there may be food in my house; Test me in this," says the LORD Almighty, "and see if I will not throw open the floodgates of heaven and pour out so much blessing that you will not have enough room for it" (Malachi 3:10).

6. Devise a plan to get out of debt and stay out.

Let me say once again, debt is not sin. But when we are in debt, we are someone else's slave. Therefore, "Let no debt remain outstanding, except the continuing debt to love one another" (Romans 13:8).

7. Avoid placing yourself under obligation to pay off someone else's debt.

Scripture counsels us to not co-sign, or put up security, for others going into debt.

> My son, if you have put up security for your neighbor, if you have struck hands in pledge for another, if you have been trapped by what you said, ensnared by the words of your mouth, then do this, my son, free yourself, since you have fallen into your neighbor's hands: Go and humble yourself.... Free yourself. (Proverbs 6:1-3, 5a).

Solomon goes on to say:

> He who puts up security for another will surely suffer, but whoever refuses to strike hands in pledge is safe (Proverbs 11:15).

8. Take decisive action.

Maybe by now you're saying, "I agree, I agree, getting out of debt is the ideal, but it's easier said than done." You're right! But here is a practical way to do it.

First, do the radical thing. Destroy every consumer credit card you have.

Don't touch them again until you are completely out of debt.

Second, before you make another purchase, ask yourself, "Is there any way I can go without this a little longer until I'm out of debt?"

Third, if you still owe a lot on your car, look into selling it and buying a less expensive used car.

Fourth, do whatever you can do to lower your monthly rent and other expenses.

Fifth, if you eat out three or four times weekly, cut back to once a week.

Take whatever drastic steps you need to take to get out of debt as soon as you can.

None of this is possible without going to God in prayer. Don't expect to be set free from financial bondage without praying about it earnestly. Pray for wisdom, prudence, and a sense of frugality. In your prayers, be willing to repeatedly affirm that all you have is the Lord's.

The following prayer is a good place to start:

Lord, all that I am, and all that I have, is Yours. I own nothing, lay claim to nothing, and fully confess that you hold the final deed to everything. Grant me wisdom to know how to manage what You have entrusted to my care. I commit myself to tithe, offering back to You at least ten percent of all that comes to me. In Jesus' name, Amen.

■ ■ ■ ■ ■

More biblical counsel

MATTHEW 25:14-30

PROVERBS 3:5-6

PHILIPPIANS 4:19

LUKE 12:15, 34

PROVERBS 11:24-25

2 CORINTHIANS 8:1-7

2 CORINTHIANS 9:6-11

MARK 12:41-42
HAGGAI 1:2-11
2 SAMUEL 24:18-25

Food Addiction

But the fruit of the
Spirit is...self-control.
GALATIANS 5:22-23

■ ■ ■ ■ ■

G lib and judgmental answers are often given to people with overeating problems: answers like, "Quit eating!" Sorry, the solution isn't quite that simple.

Unless someone is terribly overweight or has been obese in the past, he or she cannot fully identify with the pain someone with a food addiction goes through. It is a pain felt in many areas of that person's life.

Ramone sat across from me at an outside lunch bar. After we exchanged greetings, his smile too quickly disappeared. "It's obvious why I asked you to meet with me. As you can see, I'm totally out of control when it comes to eating."

At that time, Ramone weighed more than four hundred pounds! Even though he was only thirty-three, he moved like an eighty-year-old man, panting with every step he took.

It turned out that Ramone's father had abandoned the family shortly after Ramone was born. His mother remarried. Since Ramone and his younger brother didn't fit into her new plans, the boys went to live with their grandmother. As their grandmother was a widow herself, both boys missed the presence of a man in the house. They also missed discipline in almost every area of their lives.

Ramone's question to me was, "What do I do? Is there any hope for me? Am I locked in this bondage the rest of my life?" His hurt ran deep, deeper than I had first realized.

Ramone's situation is far from unique. Some 20 to 30 percent of all Americans are significantly overweight. Almost 20 percent of Americans are currently involved in some kind of weight-loss program, some on their fourth or fifth try. Makers of diet foods, pills, and exercise programs gross more than $10 billion per year!

Why are some people totally out of control with their eating? Several reasons stand out:

1. Overeating is a way of escape for some.

One overweight man confided that he ate almost continuously to escape the huge financial pressures bearing down on his business. He relied on food—especially sweets late at night—to get his mind off the constant concerns about how to stave off bankruptcy.

Many women eat excessively to escape unhappy marriages. Many wheelchair bound people eat to forget the fact that they will probably never walk again. Others who are physically scarred or otherwise marred eat to forget about their appearance.

2. Overeating is often an attempt to cover a guilt-ridden conscience.

Unfortunately, some people gorge as a denial technique, attempting to hide their guilt from others, even from themselves. Eating becomes a substitute, albeit a poor substitute, for facing and dealing with guilt caused by unresolved sin.

One woman confided that she would rather be large than try to deal with the guilt caused from her past, when she was illicitly involved with a man not her husband.

3. Much overeating results from a skewed self-image.

Though the Bible makes it clear we're not to think of ourselves more highly than we ought to think (Romans 12:3), God never intended that we go around downgrading ourselves and feeling a sense of worthlessness.

True, in order to come to Christ and be saved, we must acknowledge our utter and total depravity, confess our sin, and admit that we can't save ourselves because we're sinners. But once we've accepted Christ, we become somebody in God's eyes!

4. Overeating is sometimes a coping mechanism when everything else is out of control in a person's life.

Most people addicted to food find themselves undisciplined in other areas of their lives, as well. They find it difficult to get up early, get things done on time, or have any kind of consistent schedule in their lives. In most cases, they are people whose lives are completely out of control. Self-discipline is missing.

5. Some overeat out of nervous energy.

Those with a "hyper" personality often find themselves smoking one cigarette after another, constantly drinking a glass of something, or snacking and eating almost non-stop. This is perhaps why many people who give up smoking gain weight rather rapidly. Used to having something in their hands (namely a cigarette), they feel a compulsion to continue having something in their hands and turn to food. Soon, they become addicted to food and cannot stop.

6. Overeating may stem from one's childhood.

For some who grew up in poverty, sudden access to an abundance of food as an adult is more than they can handle, and they get into the habit of gluttony.

Others, while growing up, learned to always clean their plates, and to have seconds to finish up any leftovers. This also may cause overeating later in life.

7. Overeating masks some people's pain.

For still others, food fills a void, not just a physical hunger. It dulls the pain of their loneliness, and gives them a sense of temporary pleasure.

If those are some of the reasons someone may start overeating, why in the world would anyone keep right on overeating after becoming extremely overweight?

In a word, *denial*.

I suppose all of us have been in denial about something in our lives. Food addicts, however, usually have a serious problem here, because they fear to admit they are addicted to something will cause others to think less of them.

Most food addicts already feel badly about themselves, but withdraw into denial rather than face what others might think of them. They brush off any attempts by friends or loved ones to confront their problem. How? By justifying their situation:

- "I'm not really that much overweight, I'm just big-boned."
- "I've got a glandular problem I've struggled with for years."
- "I'm under a little stress right now, and I always eat more when the pressure gets to me."

But to come out and say, "I have an addiction to food, and it's beyond my own ability to do anything about it," seems almost impossible for some.

Making such an admission goes against their strong desire to be accepted and liked by others. It is as if they hope that denying their problems will cause others not to notice them.

HOW DO I KNOW IF I'M ADDICTED?

Here are a series of questions you need to ask yourself:

- Do you find yourself often thinking about food?
- Do you anticipate eating long before your next meal?
- Do you tend to eat when you're bored?
- Do you hide food in your desk or drawer at work? At home?
- Do you try to cover how much you take out of the refrigerator?
- Do you look forward to functions that have food more than functions that don't?
- Do you find yourself lying to others about how much you eat?
- Are you disgusted with your physical appearance?
- Do you find yourself postponing a plan to do something about your addiction?

If you answer "yes" to many of these questions, you may have a serious addiction to food.

COUNSEL FROM GOD'S WORD

Is there hope? Yes!

1. Acknowledge that you are in over your head.

In other words, confess that you have an addiction to food and that—in and of yourself—you cannot get a victory in this area. Acknowledge you need the intervening hand of God.

Ian Thomas once said:

> I can't, but You never said I could; You can, and You always said
> You could.

That's a good prayer to pray when your back is against the wall. Go back and read the story of Jehoshaphat. When he had his back against the wall, and the ensuing enemy was ready to decimate him and his army, he gladly confessed to God:

> "For we have no power to face this vast army that is attacking us.
> We do not know what to do, but our eyes are on you"
> (2 Chronicles 20:12b).

Remember, you can't break this addiction by your own will power. The apostle Paul said it well: "I can do everything through him who gives me strength" (Philippians 4:13).

2. Acknowledge that your addiction is sin.

Don't attempt to dismiss the spiritual nature of your problem, as if it were only psychological or physiological. It is a spiritual problem that demands a spiritual solution. Why? Because you've allowed something (in this case, a food addiction) to gain control of part of your life. This is clearly a violation of Scripture. Paul put it succinctly:

> Everything is permissible for me...but I will not be mastered by
> anything. Food for the stomach, and the stomach for food, but
> God will destroy them both (1 Corinthians 6:12-13).

147

As believers, we're not to be mastered by anything or anyone except Jesus Christ. Peter reminds us that "a man is a slave to whatever has mastered him" (2 Peter 2:19b). Paul adds that "sin shall not be your master" (Romans 6:14).

Addiction to anything—including food—is sin. If we want deliverance God's way, we need to confess it as sin (1 John 1:9) and repent (Acts 3:19). Repenting means changing our actions.

3. Take steps to show the sincerity of your repentance.

This means God expects some action from us. John the Baptist urged people to "produce fruit in keeping with repentance" (Matthew 3:8).

This gets into the obedience department. What specifically are we to do if we have a food addiction? For one thing, we need to avoid those occasions that bring us together with those who eat much and often.

> Do not join those who drink too much wine or gorge themselves
> on meat, for drunkards and gluttons become poor, and drowsi-
> ness clothes them in rags (Proverbs 23:20-21).

God expects us to take some action. Diets are not the answer, because diets are not where the problem lies. It lies in a person's attitude toward food. We need to heed the advice of Solomon again:

> When you sit to dine with a ruler, note well what is before you,
> and put a knife to your throat if you are given to gluttony
> (Proverbs 23:1-2).

With God's power, we need to begin to take charge of our life. We need to learn to eat to live, not live to eat.

4. Find someone to whom you can be totally accountable.

You need a Paul in your life who will mentor you and ask the hard questions, keeping your feet to the fire. You need a Nathan, who came to David and told him: "You are the man."

You may ask, "Is this scriptural?"

The answer is "yes!" All Christians are to "Submit to one another out of reverence to Christ" (Ephesians 5:21). That doesn't simply mean to be humble before one another, it means we're to confess our sins to each other (James 5:16). That's accountability.

5. Spend much time in Bible study and prayer.

Allow meditation and obedience to God's Word to be your food, in a sense. Jesus once said, "I have food to eat that you know nothing about" (John 4:32). He spoke these words when His disciples encouraged him to eat some food. Jesus implied by this statement that He derived His satisfaction from the work God had called Him to do. Jesus wasn't saying it isn't good to eat, but He was saying that we sometimes place too much emphasis on food.

One of the amazing effects of God's Word dwelling in us is that it changes our affections and brings them in line with the God's heart.

6. Do your best to avoid social events where large amounts of food are served.

Our culture celebrates eating. Almost every social function and business transaction is done over breakfast, lunch, or dinner. Avoid smorgasbord, cafeterias, buffets, and parties until your self-discipline is what it needs to be.

Paul put it this way: "do not give the devil a foothold" (Ephesians 4:27). Why? Because Satan is always trying to outwit us by one scheme or another (2 Corinthians 2:10). You need to make sure you don't invite temptation by browsing at a bakery, or by feeling you need to try out every new restaurant in town.

7. Remember God is stronger than any temptation.

Everyone is tempted to live beneath his highest and best. People with addictions can easily lose heart, thinking the thing that lures them into sin is somehow stronger than God Himself. But don't forget:

No temptation has seized you, except whatis common to man.
And God is faithful; he will not let you be tempted beyond what
you can bear. But when you are tempted he will also provide a
way out so that you can stand up under it (1 Corinthians 10:13).

This verse tells us three things about temptation. First, temptations come to one and all. Second, the lure of temptation will never be stronger than the Lord. Finally, there always is a way to escape temptation.

If you are addicted to food, and feeling guilty because you are terribly overweight, let me encourage you to start by turning your problem over—once and for all—to the Lord.

You might want to pray a prayer like this:

Lord, I confess to You that I am addicted to food. I am out of control when it comes to satisfying my appetite. Furthermore, in and of myself, I am powerless to break this addiction. I turn this addiction completely over to You, and claim Your power to enable my behavior to change. In Jesus' name, Amen.

■ ■ ■ ■ ■

More biblical counsel

MATTHEW 4:1-11
PROVERBS 25:16
PROVERBS 28:7
PROVERBS 3:5-6
PSALM 23
ISAIAH 54:17
ISAIAH 45:5-6
PHILIPPIANS 4:19
REVELATION 12:10-11
JEREMIAH 32:17
JEREMIAH 32:26
JEREMIAH 33:3

Gambling

Then he said to them,
"Watch out! Be on your guard
against all kinds of greed;
a man's life does not consist in
the abundance of his possessions."

LUKE 12:15

* * * * *

I'll call him Curt to disguise his real identity. Curt was in his late twenties, married, with two precious children. I first came to know him through a phone call of desperation.

With a voice raspy as if he hadn't slept in days, Curt told me, "I've got to see you immediately. It's a matter of life and death."

Twenty minutes later Curt arrived, unshaven, hair disheveled, absolute fear written all across his face. He sat down and immediately burst into tears. I've rarely seen a man more desperate. "I need help! I've ruined my life, my marriage, my family, and I'm ready to take my own life."

After calming Curt down enough so he could tell me what the problem was, I sat and listened to his all-too-familiar story. At that very moment, he was being pursued by his gambling creditors for the $22,000 he owed but couldn't pay. His house was being foreclosed, the bank had taken back one car, and all their utilities had been shut off except their water. His wife had taken the kids and moved back in with her parents across town.

Not only did Curt owe a huge amount of money he couldn't begin to pay, but the gambling "organization" had vowed to kill him if he didn't pay by Wednesday. It was already late Tuesday afternoon. Curt was literally running for his life, with nowhere else to turn.

Americans spent more on gambling last year than they spent on shoes, dental care, appliances, travel, and even health insurance!

Maybe you think the culprits are all in Reno, Las Vegas, and Atlantic City. Wrong! Many billions are spent annually on state lotteries. Since 1963, when the first U.S. state lottery since the 1890s was approved in New Hampshire, Americans have developed a growing fascination and lust for gambling. Millions are addicted; thousands are penniless and depressed. In a growing number of states, people can gamble right in their own homes through video games telecast with the government's blessing. Americans are spending multiplied billions of dollars on gambling, both legal and illegal, every year.

Today there's a new breed of gamblers. Formerly, gambling was associated with prostitution, crime, and lawlessness. It's "image" is changing. Much of its stigma has been removed. It has been "legitimized" and every attempt has been made to make it a respectable and "in" thing to do.

Legitimized or not, the results are still the same. Ninety-eight percent of all gamblers win little or nothing. Some, like Curt, end up losing everything.

IS GAMBLING REALLY WRONG?

I've had so many say to me, "Show me a verse in the Bible that forbids gambling." Others have said, "All of a life is a gamble. I gamble every time I get on the freeway." Many have told me gambling is even in the Bible. Some use Acts 1:26 to say the apostles "gambled" to determine who would replace Judas Iscariot.

Actually the apostles cast lots, which they believed God sovereignly controlled. The Bible says: "The lot is cast into the lap, but its every decision is from the Lord" (Proverbs 16:33). Besides, biblical lot casting didn't involve money. The apostles weren't casting lots to make an extra buck or two, but to discern God's sovereign will. There's a big difference!

Others contend that gambling isn't all bad if part of the revenue helps fund schools, highway construction, and other worthwhile causes. Others admit gambling large amounts of money is wrong, but argue that nickel and dime gambling is all right.

Is gambling really wrong? Before we answer that, let's try to understand why people gamble.

WHY DO PEOPLE GAMBLE?

1. Some gamble to supplement their regular income.

Their goal is to raise their standard of living, or at least make ends meet. Few are successful.

2. Another group of people gamble just for "fun."

They're the small percentage of folks who arrive in Las Vegas with a set amount of money to gamble and then, once it's gone, head back home.

3. Another group of people are what I call "plodder" gamblers.

They buy one or two lotto tickets at a time, not realizing how much the odds are stacked against them winning.

4. Another group gamble compulsively and on their own cannot stop.

They will lie, steal, and cheat their own loved ones in order to gamble, always sure that, "This time I'll win."

What's the basis of all gambling? I believe it's a lust for money, a desire to get rich quick. It's a thirst that for some people only gets stronger the more money they lose.

Gambling consumes people who haven't learned what Jesus taught: "a man's life does not consist in the abundance of his possessions" (Luke 12:15).

WHY IS GAMBLING WRONG?

1. It accentuates one's lack of contentment.

The apostle Paul wrote to young Timothy:

But godliness with contentment is great gain. For we brought nothing into the world, and we can take nothing out of it. But if we have food and clothing, we will be content with that (1 Timothy 6:6-8).

Gambling awakens an ungodly "want" in people. The Bible contains warning after warning about adoring the unpossessed. In fact, the richest man who ever lived, King Solomon, wrote: "Better is a little with the fear of the Lord than great wealth with turmoil" (Proverbs 15:16).

Gambling's goal is the exact opposite of godly contentment. It creates a deep sense of discontentment with what you have, claiming you deserve better and promising that something better if you'll take a "slight" risk.

The television advertisements that promote the lottery in my state are certainly designed to create a thirst for more and better. From the amount of money poured each week into that lottery, the ads appear to be working.

2. Gambling also causes a person to yield to temptation and human desire.

Paul goes on to tell Timothy:

People who want to get rich fall into temptation and a trap, and
into many foolish and harmful desires that plunge men into ruin
and destruction (1 Timothy 6:9).

Make no mistake about it! America's deepest sin is abandoning God in our intense craving for material prosperity.

Gambling is fueled by pure greed. People may tell you they do it only as a sport, that "it's not the money." Don't believe it!

Solomon wisely observed: "A greedy man brings trouble to his family, but he who hates bribes will live" (Proverbs 15:27). He also noted: "Whoever trusts in his riches will fall" (Proverbs 11:28a).

Gamblers are convinced they're going to have a breakthrough, hit the jackpot, make it big. It's almost always an elusive dream. Again, Solomon warned:

Do not wear yourself out to get rich; have the wisdom to show
restraint. Cast but a glance at riches, and they are gone, for they
will surely sprout wings, and fly off to the sky like an eagle
(Proverbs 23:4-5).

3. Gambling promotes trust in wealth, not God.

The apostle Paul continues his warning:

> For the love of money is the root of all kinds of evils. Some people, eager for money, have wandered from the faith and pieced themselves with many griefs (1 Timothy 6:10).

Notice, Paul doesn't say that money itself is the root of evil. The *love* of money is the problem! When a person gambles, he is placing his trust in mere wealth to provide his needs. Little does he realize, "Whoever trusts in his riches will fall, but the righteous will thrive like a green leaf" (Proverbs 11:28).

The prophet Jeremiah warned the Israelites concerning placing their trust elsewhere, not in the Lord:

> Cursed is the one who trusts in man, who depends on flesh for his strength, and whose heart turns away from the Lord. He will be like a bush in the wastelands; he will not see prosperity when it comes. He will dwell in the parched places of the desert, in a salt land where no one lives. But blessed is the man who trusts in the Lord, whose confidence is in him. He will be like a tree planted by the water that sends out its roots by the stream. It does not fear when heat comes; its leaves are always green. It has no worry in the year of drought, and never fails to bear fruit" (Jeremiah 17:5-8).

Gambling maximizes man's trust in money, and minimizes his trust in God. How foolish! "The blessing of the Lord brings wealth, and he adds no trouble to it" (Proverbs 10:22).

Even wealth gained righteously isn't the greatest thing in life. Solomon certainly knew that: "A good name is more desirable than great riches; to be esteemed is better than silver or gold" (Proverbs 22:1). In several of His parables, Jesus went a step further: a right relationship with God is most desirable of all!

Gambling is sin because it promotes trusting one's "luck," not the sovereignty of God. The Bible instructs us to depend on God, who "will meet all your needs, according to his glorious riches in Christ Jesus" (Philippians 4:19).

4. Gambling denies the fact that money is temporal at best.

Again, I quote the apostle Paul's words to young Timothy:

Command those who are rich in this present world not to be arrogant, nor to put their hope in wealth, which is so uncertain, but to
put their hope in God, who richly provides us with everything for
our enjoyment (1 Timothy 6:17).

Solomon also had a graphic way of reminding us what the future holds
for those whose whole aim in life is to get rich:

A stingy man is eager to get rich and is unaware that poverty
awaits him (Proverbs 28:22).

5. Gambling is wrong because it entices you to gain money at the expense of others.

In gambling, someone may win, but only at the expense of other people.
To gain money from a system that puts someone else in financial straights is the
same as stealing. Someone beat Curt out of $22,000, depriving his family of
funds they desperately needed to live. Gambling is nothing more than organized theft.

6. Gambling confirms the location of our heart's affection.

In His sermon on the mount, Jesus laid down a very important principle
concerning money: "For where your treasure is, there will your heart be also"
(Matthew 6:21). If our treasure is bet on the horses, or football games, or the
lottery, we're not pulling the wool over the Lord's eyes. He knows exactly where
our heart is.

If we are fully and totally committed as disciples of Jesus Christ, a large
amount of our treasure will be invested to "seek first his kingdom and his righteousness" (Matthew 6:33).

When Curt talked to me about his gambling problem, he confessed he
had not given one dime to kingdom work since he began gambling. How could
he? Or, better, why would he want to? Instead of following Jesus, he was chas-
ing the wind.

7. Gambling is a sin because it promotes idolatry.

People who gamble may disagree, but it's true. Gamblers who speak fondly of Lady Luck or Dame Fortune aren't just using colorful words. They're "bowing the knee" at her shrine.

Most gamblers believe in luck, and have some way of picking what they think are "lucky" numbers. They honestly think there is some mystic force (not God) directing the roll of the dice. Such beliefs are nothing more than superstition, nothing different from avoiding black cats, walking around ladders, and bemoaning every Friday the thirteenth.

8. Gambling kills all compassion and concern for other people.

Ask any gambler who is hooked. He will tell you that since being hooked on gambling, he has lost all affection for his spouse, family, friends, co-workers. A ruthless "win or else" attitude takes precedence over everything. Such a person becomes inward, selfish, tight, and arrogant. Gambling never betters a person's character; it only worsens it.

9. Gambling creates a false hope that always disappoints.

Several years ago, the Pennsylvania lottery reached a record-breaking jackpot of $100 million. It set off a gambling mania all over the country. A total of 24 million tickets were sold in a few days. The odds that any one person would win were one in 9.6 million! Yet people continued to buy millions of tickets, literally throwing their money away. One man reportedly bought $50,000 worth of tickets in a single day!

Many foolishly gamble to pay off old gambling debts, only digging a deeper hole for themselves.

WHAT ABOUT CURT?

Curt's problem certainly didn't disappear overnight. We were able to cut off all contact between him and the gambling "organization," however, thanks to a group of Christian men who advanced Curt the money needed to pay off his huge gambling debt.

After he deeply repented of his sin, Curt was placed with a mentor, who met with him twice weekly for almost a year. Through intense discipleship and

Scripture memorization, he was soon on his way to becoming a man of God. After proving he was serious about breaking his addiction, Curt was reconciled to his wife a few months later.

Today, Curt has a good job, he already has paid back about $19,000 of the money advanced by the group, and his gambling days are history. He now counsels other young men struggling with the same problem he had.

Curt's story almost didn't have a happy ending. Just as easily, I could have had to report that he was murdered at the age of twenty-nine, leaving behind a wife and two small children. By God's grace Curt escaped. Not everyone does.

STEPS TO FREEDOM

Are you addicted to gambling? Does it have you by the throat? If so, I urge you to carefully review the detailed biblical counsel given above. Then take these practical steps.

1. Stop gambling immediately and pay off your existing gambling debts as quickly as you can (Proverbs 28:13).

2. Confess to God that what you've done is sin, and claim His forgiveness (1 John 1:9).

3. Admit that in and of yourself, you cannot break your addiction to gambling and must rely on God's power (Romans 7:14).

4. Set aside one hour daily, early in the morning, to have a meaningful, quiet time of prayer and Bible study (Psalm 5:1-3).

Keep a spiritual diary of your daily readings, prayers, and impressions.

5. Find a friend who will be tough with you, to whom you can be accountable (James 5:16).

Give him permission to ask the hard questions. Maybe this friend needs to disciple you for a year. Ask him to pray with and for you in your presence weekly—more often, if possible.

6. Get a new set of friends that in no way includes any of your old gambling cronies.

The Bible clearly says: "Bad company corrupts good character" (1 Corinthians 15:33). You cannot expect to be victorious over this sin until you completely change your associations. You may need to move to another state so that all ties can be cut off. Don't hesitate to do that if necessary.

7. Apologize and ask the forgiveness of those you've hurt by your gambling (Matthew 5:23-24).

Be especially sensitive to your spouse and your children. Ask them to be patient with you while you rebuild your life. Talk to your pastor about how your gambling has hurt the local church. Go to your other creditors, admit to them why you haven't paid your bills, then explain you have a plan to start paying them, month by month, slowly but surely.

8. Begin to tithe of your income to your local church again (Malachi 3:10-11).

Make sure your giving is consistent, not spasmodic or haphazard (1 Corinthians 16:1-2).

9. Avoid gambling of any kind,

even pitching pennies, buying a raffle ticket, or betting a steak dinner on the outcome of a ball game. This will set a great example for your children.

Even if you're seriously addicted to gambling, there is hope. Like Curt, you can turn to God today.

■ ■ ■ ■ ■

More biblical counsel

EXODUS 20:15
EXODUS 20:17
2 KINGS 5:1-27
COLOSSIANS 3:1-6

ROMANS 12:1

1 PETER 5:6-7

2 PETER 2:19

2 PETER 3:11-12

1 CORINTHIANS 10:31

1 CORINTHIANS 6:12

1 CORINTHIANS 6:9-10

PHILIPPIANS 4:8

EPHESIANS 4:17-32

EPHESIANS 6:10-20

JAMES 5:1-6

ACTS 5:1-11

HEBREWS 13:5

Grief

Weeping may remain for a night,
but rejoicing comes in the morning.
PSALMS 30:5

▪ ▪ ▪ ▪ ▪

One of my close friends was forty-three, healthy, vibrant, full of life. He loved the Lord with all his heart and pastored a dynamic, growing church in the southwest part of the country. On one occasion I called him up, inviting him to speak for me one Sunday evening, then teach for four days at the graduate school of which I serve as president.

That Sunday afternoon, his car suddenly careened out of control and hit a concrete abutment. It was a horrible accident. He suffered massive injuries, was rushed to a nearby hospital, and soon thereafter died.

I found myself comforting my friend's grief-stricken wife, who had made the trip to Seattle with him. It seemed so unreal to all of us. She lost a dear husband, their son lost his father, his mother lost a son, a church in Tucson lost a beloved pastor, and I lost one of my closest friends. One minute he was on his way to Overlake, the next moment he was on his way to heaven. It all happened so fast. I wasn't even able to get to the hospital in time.

I found myself breaking into tears for days, even weeks after his death. Grief came to me and others like a vicious knife—sudden, terrifying, painful, penetrating—creating wounds that would take a long time to heal.

Grief is an intense emotion. It encompasses all the different pain and sorrow we feel after a tragic, personal loss.

STAGES OF GRIEF

While degrees of emotion vary from person to person, grief almost always runs this course:

1. Initial shock.

This is the moment when the news first comes, either over the phone or in person. Sometimes this initial shock leaves the survivor stunned, numb to the huge surge of feelings rushing in all at once.

One mother told me that when she answered her front door at 2:00 A.M. and saw a highway patrolman standing there with a sober face, she instantly knew—her son was gone. Sure enough, no matter how he carefully couched the words, the patrolman had to break the news to her that her nineteen-year-old son had lost his life in a head-on collision after drinking. The news left her paralyzed, almost without any visible emotion at first. The tears didn't start flowing until later.

2. A time of uncontrollable weeping.

This seems always to follow. No matter how strained a relationship with a loved one may have been, after tragedy strikes we feel an overwhelming sense of loss. There is no opportunity to make everything right, to say one last good-bye.

Tears flow like a river.

3. A sense of guilt and regret.

The survivor thinks, "If I had only done this or that, it wouldn't have happened." Self-blame sets in almost immediately. I certainly experienced this: "If only I hadn't invited my friend to come visit, he'd still be alive."

Yet the Scriptures consistently teach that the days of our life are numbered, predetermined by God Himself. Moses prayed: "Teach us to number our days aright that we may gain a heart of wisdom" (Psalm 90:12).

In his sorrow, Job affirmed this when he prayed:

Man's days are determined; you have decreed the number of his months, and have set limits he cannot exceed (Job 14:5).

Thinking of this same truth, David thanked God:

All the days ordained for me were written in your book before one of them came to be. How precious to me are your thoughts, O God. How vast is the sum of them! (Psalm 139:16-17).

4. Feelings of anger toward God.

"What have I done to deserve this? If God is really all-powerful, why did He permit this to happen to my loved one?" Such intense emotion emerges partly out of frustration, partly in defense of the deceased.

Normally, such anger doesn't last long. Scripture warns:

In your anger do not sin. Do not let the sun go down while you are still angry, and do not give the devil a foothold (Ephesians 4:26-27).

5. A spirit of defeatism.

"I just can't go on without him," a woman once said to me several weeks after her husband's sudden death. Listless, apathetic, she had almost completely lost interest in life. Nothing excited her anymore.

Many will go into an extended state of grief, withdrawing and cutting off almost all social contacts. Hopefully, this period is short, however.

6. The period of healing.

This is the period of admitting one's loss and starting the journey of adjusting to it. As sudden and tragic as death always is, the survivor realizes the daily functions of life must go on.

During this period larger changes must be made: the final disposition of the clothes and personal effects of the deceased, perhaps the sale of a house, possibly the move to another city or state.

LEARNING FROM GRIEF

If a reasonable period of time has passed and you are still in the depths of sorrow, remember that grief can teach us some very valuable lessons.

Robert Hamilton wrote:

I walked a mile with pleasure,
She chatted all the way,
But left me none the wiser
For all she had to say.

I walked a mile with sorrow,
And ne'er a word said she;
But Oh, the things I learned from her
When sorrow walked with me.

How true! While we learn little from bliss, we can learn much from sorrow. But what are some of the lessons to be learned?

1. Sorrow serves as a reminder of the brevity of life.

Whether we live "three score and ten" years or are taken in the prime of life, life is always too brief. Someone has rightly observed that life is a moment between two eternities, a grain of sand on God's vast shore, a brief intermission between long acts.

James put it this way:

What is your life? You are a mist that appears for a little while and then vanishes (James 4:14b).

Stacked against the spectrum of eternity, the few years we have here on earth are but a moment. We need to be reminded of that so we don't become lax, but rather stay useful for God.

2. Sorrow drives us to our knees.

The poet was right when he wrote: "When sorrow comes, as come it must, In God a man must put his trust." Those words by John Greenleaf Whittier flowed out of his own first-hand experience with sorrow.

One man who lost his wife of thirty-five years recently told me, "Pastor, I've never prayed so much in all my life as I have in the last three months." In talking more, he divulged to me how much closer to the Lord her passing had brought him.

3. Sorrow equips us to help others who grieve.

Until you have graduated from the University of Grief, you cannot fully comfort others who go through sorrow. The apostle Paul put it this way:

> Praise be to the God and Father of our Lord Jesus Christ, the
> Father of compassion and the God of all comfort, who com-
> forts us in all our trouble, so that we can comfort those in
> any trouble with the comfort we ourselves have received from
> God (2 Corinthians 1:3-4).

When you have walked through the valley of a loved one's death, you're uniquely qualified to comfort others who are going through the same thing.

I know a woman who prayed to God when her husband died, "Lord, use this in my life to bless other people somehow." Little did she know that God would lead her to a ministry of grief support that has already blessed hundreds.

4. Grief compels us to rely on God, not ourselves.

Of all the lessons grief teaches us, this is perhaps the most poignant of all. The depths of grief can be extremely low. Yet it's when we're at our lowest that God teaches us we cannot survive without Him.

When the apostle Paul had cried until he could cry no more, he wrote what I think are some of the most beautiful words of Scripture:

> We were under great pressure, far beyond our ability to endure, so that we despaired even of life. Indeed, in our hearts we felt the sentence of death. But this happened that we might not rely on ourselves, but on God who raises the dead (2 Corinthians 1:8b-9).

Paul realized God had allowed this period of sorrow, if for no other reason, to drive him to reliance on the Lord instead of himself. This indeed is one of the lessons and blessings of grief.

By now, you may be asking, "How can I move beyond this smothering grief?" I believe the following steps will make a difference in your life.

COUNSEL FROM GOD'S WORD

1. Know that God understands and cares about your grief.

No one cried more than David when told of the death of Absalom, his son. He felt so devastated that, at first, he couldn't bring himself to join in celebrating the tremendous victory his army has just secured.

Yet David knew his God, and wrote: "Record my lament, list my tears on your scroll—are they not in your record?" (Psalm 56:8). Older versions read, "...put my tears in thy bottle...." When I used to read that, I thought God must have a lot of bottles to be able to put all the world's tears in them.

The promise of God never fails: "The LORD is close to the brokenhearted and saves those who are crushed in spirit" (Psalm 34:18). He knows, He cares, and He will act.

Jesus wept at the tomb of Lazarus, His friend. He knows what it is to experience loss, and is more than able to help us when we're walking through that valley.

2. Ask God to turn your sorrow into joy.

That may sound impossible, but this is what Scripture actually teaches. Just before Jesus left His disciples and went to the cross, He said:

> "I tell you the truth, you will weep and mourn while the world rejoices. You will grieve, but your grief will turn to joy. A woman giving birth to a child has pain, because her time has come; but when her baby is born she forgets the anguish because of her joy that a baby is born into the world. So with you; Now is your time of grief, but I will see you again, and you will rejoice, and no one will take away your joy" (John 16:20-22).

Notice what Jesus said: "your grief will turn to joy." He didn't say: "your grief will be *replaced* by joy." No, the very thing that brought grief because of pain is the same thing that later brings joy.

What happens? God creates a metamorphosis. He takes the very source of our sorrow, and turns it into joy—if we let Him.

3. Review the wonderful memories you have of your loved one.

Death may snatch your loved one away, but it cannot rob you of the wonderful memories you have. Bring those memories to mind from time to time. Paul wrote:

> Finally, brothers, whatever is true, whatever is noble, whatever is right, whatever is pure, whatever is lovely, whatever is admirable—if anything is excellent or praiseworthy—think about such things (Philippians 4:8).

There is no area of life where this is more applicable than in the loss of a loved one. Cherish memories of good times, of goals reached together, of the birth of your children, of birthdays, of anniversaries, and of other happy times.

I know a woman who compiled a scrapbook titled, "Our Life Together, Wonderful Memories." On cold rainy nights, she would play the music she and her deceased husband had enjoyed together and go through the scrapbook. Tears? Yes, there were a few, but she told me there were more smiles and a fond re-living of the good times they had together. She took Philippians 4:8 to heart, and it worked!

4. Spend more time praising God.

Praise and worship of God ward off sorrow and sadness.
Isaiah realized this when he spoke of

...beauty instead of ashes, the oil of gladness instead of
mourning, and a garment of praise instead of a spirit of
despair (Isaiah 61:3b).

When Jonah was in the belly of the fish, grieving over his disobedience, he began to praise God. Soon thereafter God caused the great fish to vomit out Jonah onto dry land!

When Paul and Silas were severely beaten and then thrown in jail for preaching the gospel, they were in great pain and sorrow. But instead of wallowing in their grief, they began to sing praises to the Lord. At midnight, God caused a great earthquake, opening all the jail doors.

In your own times of grief, sing praises to God. Especially go back through Psalms 95-150, rehearsing all the great praise passages.

5. Get involved immediately in ministering to others.

Becoming a servant to others has a way of dissolving the cutting grief in our own lives. Paul reminded the Ephesians, "Serve wholeheartedly, as if you were serving the Lord, not men" (Ephesians 6:7).

For one thing, when we're busy ministering in some way to others in the church, we don't have time for self-pity. Beyond that, pouring our lives into others is therpeutic. As we serve others, we ourselves are blessed.

Jesus taught that true greatness comes from serving others:

"Whoever wants to become great among you must be your servant, and whoever wants to be first must be slave of all. For even the Son of Man did not come to be served, but to serve, and to give his life as a ransom for many" (Mark 10:43b-45).

It is in ministering to others that we realize our full potential as human beings.

6. Get on with your life.

I know that may sound trite, but it's true. Paul himself said: "one thing I do: Forgetting what is behind, and straining toward what is ahead, I press on" (Philippians 3:13). That's what God wants you to do, too.

In order to do this effectively, you need to set some vocational, educational, or other goals. The longer you put off moving back into the main stream of life, the harder it will be to do it.

There is a legitimate time to grieve, but then we need to move ahead. Solomon wrote there is:

A time to weep and a time to laugh, a time to mourn and a time to dance (Ecclesiastes 3:4).

7. Find your strength in the Lord.

Friends are wonderful, relatives are helpful, and co-workers are kind and compassionate. They all fill a very important role when we're going through the agony of grief. But ultimately, you need to find your strength in the Lord.

A good example of this is recorded in 1 Samuel 30. The Amalekites had raided the town of Ziklag, burned it, and taken captive all who were there. When David and his army arrived at Ziklag, they saw the horrible carnage and devastation. They grieved for their wives and children. Scripture says: "David and his men wept aloud until they had no strength left to weep" (1 Samuel 30:4).

That's serious grieving! To make matters worse, some talked of stoning David. It was surely his lowest hour, the loneliest time of his life. But the Bible says: "David found strength in the LORD his God" (1 Samuel 30:6b).

He didn't find strength in his army, his weapons, his clever strategies, or his own strength, but in the Lord. What a testimony! It's no wonder David later said, "The LORD is the stronghold of my life" (Psalm 27:1).

By now you may be wondering how I handled the loss of a best friend. It wasn't easy, but knowing he is in heaven and knowing the day of our death is appointed by the Lord, I've rested my case with God's sovereignty.

Do I miss my friend? More than I can express. But I've frequently rehearsed the precious memories of our close relationship. I recall the places we went, the conferences we enjoyed together, the times we knelt and prayed for each other, the times we literally wept together. To this day, those memories continue to help me work through my loss.

Remember that grief doesn't last forever. David wrote: "weeping may remain for a night, but rejoicing comes in the morning" (Psalm 30:5).

■ ■ ■ ■ ■

More biblical counsel

PHILIPPIANS 4:19

2 CORINTHIANS 5:1

1 CORINTHIANS 15

JOHN 11:25-26

JAMES 1:2-4

PSALM 62:1

PSALM 90

PSALM 91

ISAIAH 40:1-11

ISAIAH 40:28-31

ISAIAH 63:7-9

Job 14:1-14
Job 19:23-27
2 Samuel 12:16-23
Romans 8:31-39
2 Corinthians 4:5-18
1 Thessalonians 4:13-18
Revelation 21
Hebrews 11:1-10

Homosexuality

Then the Lord God made a
woman from the rib he had
taken out of the man, and he
brought her to the man.

GENESIS 2:22

■■■■■

"Can I be a practicing homosexual and still consider myself a Christian?" The young man asking me that question over the phone wished to remain anonymous. But since I have a policy of not counseling over the phone without knowing someone's name, I soon learned his name was John.

Later, I met John in person. Only twenty-seven, his life already had been marred by much heartache and pain.

An older cousin had molested John between his seventh and fifteenth years. John also had a violent and physically abusive father, with whom he had virtually no relationship.

By the time he was seventeen, John was out of the house, living here and there with friends and one relative. He ended up falling in with the wrong crowd of guys and by the time he was twenty, John was "street-wise" in a world of homosexuality. He confided in me that he had probably had well over one hundred sexual partners.

Through the witness of a bus driver, John repented of his past, gave his heart to the Lord, and started going to church. In spite of his high resolve to leave his twisted and perverted lifestyle, and remain celibate until marriage, John fell back into sexual sin before finishing his first month as a new Christian.

Guilt-laden, ashamed, depressed, and tempted to believe "once a homosexual, always a homosexual," John called me.

I think John knew the answer to the question he asked me over the phone, but because of propaganda he had received from some of his so-called "Christian" homosexual friends, he was confused.

In the past two decades there has been a dramatic rise in the public's awareness of homosexuality. By attempting to take away some of the stigma of homosexuality and make it simply an "alternate lifestyle," gay rights advocates have made significant strides in "legitimizing" the practice of homosexuality. In many ways, they have been successful in getting people to talk about the issues of rights and discrimination, not the issue of morality.

Little did anyone think at the time that the civil rights movement of the fifties and sixties would later be applied to homosexuals. Traditionally, "minorities" in our country have been defined by race, creed, color, or national origin. Homosexuals have sought to change all of that to include behavior-based groups, specifically homosexuals.

Part of the push has been to grant homosexuals protected status in the military, as public school teachers, as Boy Scout leaders, and as adoptive parents, as well as to convince people that homosexuality is genetic, not a life-style of choice. This latter is an attempt to remove the guilt of homosexuality, raising its practice to a new level of acceptability and respectability.

Another ploy has been to convince our culture that a large percentage of the American population—10 percent, it was said—is homosexual. This was based in part on research done by Dr. Alfred Kinsey and his associates several decades ago. His estimate was skewed by the fact that many of the men he surveyed were incarcerated at the time; the percentage of homosexuals in prison is normally much higher than the national average.

Current estimates by reputable national pollsters place the number of homosexuals in our country at between 1.5 to 2 percent. Furthermore, geneticists in no way have uniformly and convincingly found evidence proving homosexuality is an inherited trait, let alone simply a matter of genetics.

Beyond biology, sociology, politics, and public relations, however, let's take an honest, scriptural look at the morality of homosexual behavior.

IS HOMOSEXUAL BEHAVIOR REALLY SINFUL?

The overwhelming evidence of Scripture says "yes."

Genesis 19 tells what happened when two angels appeared as men and went to the home of Lot, warning him to flee the city before God destroyed it. Scripture says the homosexual men of the city came and demanded to have homosexual relations with Lot's guests. Lot offered his daughters, but the gang of men demanded that Lot turn over his guests to their wicked designs. God destroyed the city that next morning, judging "sodomy" most severely.

Some homosexual advocates have tried to write off this passage by saying God destroyed the city of Sodom because of some other sins, not homosexuality. True, the Sodomites were guilty of many despicable deeds. But Scripture specifically says God judged the city for its rampant homosexuality.

In Old Testament times, there was no question what God thought of homosexuality. He had commanded: "Do not lie with a man as one lies with a woman; that is detestable" (Leviticus 18:22). The penalty for violating that command also was made very clear:

If a man lies with a man as one lies with a woman, both of them have done what is detestable. They must be put to death; their blood will be on their own heads (Leviticus 20:13).

Furthermore, even the garments and other apparel of homosexuals were not allowed in the house of the Lord:

You must not bring the earrings of a female prostitute or of a male prostitute into the house of the Lord your God to pay any vow, because the Lord your God detests them both (Deuteronomy 23:18).

Male prostitutes in Old Testament times were male prostitutes for male patrons, not females. People knew exactly what God was forbidding.

Furthermore, 1 Timothy 1:8-10 teaches that the law was given not for the righteous, but for murderers, adulterers, homosexual offenders, and other ungodly people opposed to God.

In Romans 1:26-32, the apostle Paul makes it absolutely clear that homosexual behavior is a perversion. We're told in verse 26 that God gave the rebellious over to shameful lusts. He then writes:

> In the same way the men also abandoned natural relations with
> women, and were inflamed with lust for one another. Men com-
> mitted indecent acts with other men, and received in themselves
> the due penalty for their perversion (Romans 1:27).

Notice that God considers natural sex as something that occurs between a man and woman, not between individuals of the same sex. Homosexuality is unnatural, contrary to God's will and plan.

Finally, Scripture teaches that the practice of homosexuality will result in eternal condemnation unless, of course, like any sin, a person repents of it. Paul writes:

> Neither the sexually immoral, nor idolaters nor adulterers, nor
> male prostitutes, nor homosexual offenders will inherit the king-
> dom of God. And that is what some of you were. But you were
> washed, you were sanctified, you were justified in the name of the
> Lord Jesus Christ and by the Spirit of our God (1 Corinthians
> 6:9-11).

Make no mistake about it. Homosexuality isn't just another "lifestyle," it's sin, and needs to be dealt with the same way any other sin is dealt with.

BUT CAN A HOMOSEXUAL CHANGE?

Militant, unrepentant homosexuals say "no." They claim it's ingrained, part of one's genetic makeup, and thus irreversible. If that's true, why did Paul say in 1 Corinthians 6:11—quoted above—that some of the Corinthians "were" once involved in that sin?

The use of the word "were" indicates they had been homosexuals in the past, but now were washed, sanctified, and justified. In other words, they had left their former homosexual lifestyle by trusting and following Jesus Christ.

John is a living example that the homosexual lifestyle can be changed by the power of Jesus Christ. After only six months in a Bible-based support group in our city, meeting with other ex-homosexuals, John had enough strength in the Lord to completely walk away from his old life-style. He's been out for almost four years now!

John now would say someone cannot call himself a true Christian while continuing an ungodly practice, whether homosexuality, adultery, or whatever. After all, darkness and light, sin and obedience don't go together.

COUNSEL FROM GOD'S WORD

If you have been or presently are involved in homosexuality, I urge you to take the following steps.

1. Understand that God loves you and gave His Son, Jesus Christ, to die for all your sins.

Even though God deplores your sin, His first desire isn't to judge you, but rather to redeem you (John 3:16; 2 Peter 3:9).

2. Repent and confess your sin to God.

Call your behavior what it is, rebellion against God (Luke 13:3, Acts 17:30, 2 Corinthians 7:10).

3. Find a confidant and confess your sin to him.

Select someone you know you can trust, someone spiritually mature who has experience biblically counseling others (James 5:16).

4. Find a discipler or mentor to whom you can be accountable on an ongoing basis.

Grant him permission to ask the hard questions of you. David had his Nathan, Timothy had his Paul, and you need someone, too.

5. Abandon any friendship or acquaintance with someone involved in homosexuality (1 Corinthians 15:33-34, 2 Corinthians 6:14-18).

6. Change your thought patterns, developing the mind of Christ.

Ask God to "renew" your mind (Romans 12:1-2, Ephesians 4:20-24, Colossians 3:9-10).

7. Avoid watching television for at least three months, until you become stronger in the Lord.

Why subject yourself to repeated reminders of your past life-style?

8. Join an organized Bible study as soon as you can, preferably one that demands some accountability (Acts 17:11).

9. Completely avoid spending time anywhere alone with a person of the same sex at any time, for any reason.

Deal ruthlessly with sinful thoughts and deeds. Remember, we're not to give the devil any kind of "opportunity" to get a crack at us (Ephesians 4:27).

10. Remain confident that God can deliver you from your past life-style.

While homosexuality is a perversion, it should not be treated differently than immorality with someone of the opposite sex. Sin is sin, and sin of the flesh is still sin of the flesh. Remember that God can deliver people from both (Ephesians 3:20).

11. Look to God for the assurance of your salvation.

You may not practice homosexuality for months, yet still have thoughts in that direction from time to time. Does that mean you're not saved?

Remember, all Christians struggle with their thought lives, both heterosexuals and homosexuals. Colossians 3:1 tells us how we can change our thought lives: "set your hearts on things above, where Christ is seated at the right hand of God." Renounce any thoughts of sexual immorality.

God can and will deliver anyone who is willing to sell out to Jesus Christ and truly become His. Never forget the words of Scripture: we "can do everything through him who gives [us] strength" (Philippians 4:13).

· · · · ·

More biblical counsel

2 CORINTHIANS 5:17

PSALM 1

PHILIPPIANS 4:8

ROMANS 8:7-8

ROMANS 12:1-2

1 JOHN 2:28

1 JOHN 3:9

1 JOHN 4:4

REVELATION 22:14-15

Hurt

*Cast all your anxiety on him
because he cares for you.*
I PETER 5:7

■ ■ ■ ■ ■

Betty was bubbly, appeared to be on top of things, and spread cheer wherever she went. The mother of two preschoolers, she was always on the run with church activities, pre-school classes, swimming lessons, shopping, and managing a household. No one would have guessed in a hundred years that inside such a bubbly person was another Betty—with a broken heart.

Betty's mom and dad divorced when she was only twelve. During her teen years, she vowed that would never happen to her. In her late teens Betty dreamed of falling in love, getting married, having a family, and living happily ever after.

Virtually no one knew that Betty wept inside much of the time. Her husband, Rex, had become an abusive man, putting her down in front of others, complaining about everything, and privately dishing out verbal abuse that cut to the bone. I later learned Rex was hooked on pornography and had been involved in at least one affair, with strong evidence pointing to a second.

Betty couldn't bring herself to admit to her friends and relatives how badly she hurt from the rejection and abuse she had suffered. Only when there was no more room for tears on the inside did they start spilling over on the outside.

Betty mentioned she once had spilled hot grease on her foot. The pain of that burn was so intense she could barely stand it, but she said the pain she was suffering now on the inside was far worse!

I remember standing in the delivery room watching my first grandchild's birth. I found myself crying when I saw her for the first time. In retrospect I think I was crying because I could foresee all the hurt that precious girl would have to endure someday, and I wanted to somehow insulate her against all the "owies" life would hurl at her. The fact is, I can't.

When she was in first grade, my granddaughter came home from school one day bawling her eyes out because another little girl had said she was ugly. Her little heart was so broken she sobbed convulsively. Yes, she got over it, but it was only the first installment of many more hurts to come.

Solomon once wrote in Proverbs: "A man's spirit sustains him in sickness, but a crushed spirit who can bear?" (Proverbs 18:14).

There are a great many hurts people suffer. Some are described in other chapters. Nine of the most common are discussed below.

THE HURT OF LONELINESS

Researchers have found the percentage of people living alone is larger and increasing faster than at any other time in America's history. Even marketers have adjusted the size of foods, detergent, and soft drinks for this growing market segment. People are marrying about four years later now than they did in 1970. There is a greater demand than ever before for single-occupancy housing units.

With increased singleness comes increased loneliness. This isn't to say that all single men and women are lonely. The impersonalization of society compounds this sense of loneliness, thanks to drive through banking, fast foods, prescriptions, you name it. Often, we don't even see—let alone know— the individuals with whom we do business.

The number of single parents also has risen dramatically in every metropolitan area across the nation. Single parents suffer from a loneliness that is almost unbearable at times. Every time they see an unfragmented family, they're reminded of the deep hurt they must bear.

THE HURT OF BEING UNEMPLOYED

One man recently told me, "Until you've been there, you don't know how much it hurts." He had never been out of a job in his life, but in this up and down economy there have been many firsts. Not only was he out of a job, but it seemed no one wanted to employ him since he was fifty-seven years old, nearing retirement age.

Jesus told a parable about a landowner who hired men to work in his vineyard:

> "About the eleventh hour he went out and found still others
> standing around. He asked them, 'Why have you been standing
> here all day long doing nothing?' 'Because no one has hired us,'
> they answered" (Matthew 20:6-7a).

"No one has hired us"! That brief statement reveals a great deal of hurt. A day's wages have been lost. Another measure of self-esteem has been eroded.

Man was made to work productively. To stand idle is to live contrary to everything we were created for. A sense of worthlessness has a way of creeping over the unemployed.

THE HURT OF REJECTION

A sixteen-year-old hangs his head to the ground when he comes home from football practice. He didn't make the team.

An eighteen-year-old stands by the mailbox waiting to see if she was accepted at the university. She tears into the envelope, and looks at two words: "accepted" and "rejected." She sees a check mark in the box by "rejected." What a crushing blow.

A relationship is broken, and you are spurned in favor of someone else. This is one of the hardest types of rejections to take. It leaves you feeling devastated inside, like someone who is "unclean."

Rejection hurts!

THE HURT OF GRIEF

This has to be one of the most penetrating hurts of all. Friends mean well, and they try, but sometimes they simply cannot know or touch the hurt that aches so deeply inside you when a loved one has been snatched away. It's not just the grief, it's the hurt of loss that is acute. The hurt is accentuated by the permanence of it all.

I think of the hurt expressed by David when his son Absalom was killed: "O my son Absalom! If only I had died instead of you, O Absalom, my son, my son!" (2 Samuel 18:33b).

You can almost feel David's pain as he wept for his deceased son. Those of you who have lost a parent, child, spouse, or close friend certainly know the hurt doesn't easily go away.

Note: If you are grieving over the lost of a loved one, please see chapter 19.

THE HURT OF DEFEAT

Employees work extra hard to prepare a competitive bid, but the company doesn't get the job. A professional golfer nearly wins a major tournament, only to be beaten by a young upstart. A seasoned politician loses the race of his life by a narrow margin. A quarterback loses the first two games of the season after throwing a record number of interceptions.

Defeat hurts! When the children of Israel were taken into captivity, they wondered how they could sing the Lord's song in a foreign land. By their own testimony they were defeated:

There on the poplars we hung our harps, for there our captors
asked us for songs, our tormentors demanded songs of joy; they
said, "Sing us one of the songs of Zion" (Psalm 137:2-3).

You can almost hear the defeat in their words. Many have hung up their harps after a crushing defeat.

THE HURT OF BEING HANDICAPPED

I talked with a handsome young man who had become a paraplegic. When he was twenty-four, his spinal cord had been severed when his car struck a tree. Six months after his injury, I asked him how he was coping with his paralysis.

"It hurts, it really hurts!" I saw tears form in his dark brown eyes as he described how it feels each time he sees a guy his age jogging, playing golf, or dancing.

Paralysis, deafness, blindness, amputation, disfigurement from burns, an obvious birth defect, or the limitations caused by Muscular Dystrophy—whatever physical handicap you may have, deep down you've probably experienced a lot of hurt.

THE HURT OF BROKEN DREAMS

Ted and Monica dreamed of owning their own flower shop. They carefully saved, planned, skimped, and worked hard to reach specific goals.

After three years of saving every dollar they could find, Ted and Monica applied for a small business loan and were approved. They opened their shop on a bright spring day. Business was brisk for the first two or three months, then a series of misfortunes set in.

Ted became ill, the owner of their building suddenly increased their rent by 40 percent, and a supermarket with a flower shop went in next door. A severe drop in business brought a drop in profits. Soon Ted and Monica couldn't make enough to even pay the rent.

Tearfully one evening, they locked the door of their flower shop for the last time. Their lifelong dream was shattered, and the hurt they felt went deep.

THE HURT OF GUILT AND SHAME

Teel was young, married only two years, with a bright future ahead with the company for which he worked. But since his wife quit work to stay home with their new baby, finances had been tight.

Teel began to "borrow" from the till for lunch money. Then he started to "borrow" more for gas money. Soon he was embezzling between $800 and $1,000 per month, covering his tracks with clever computer programming.

Then the inevitable happened. Teel's supervisor asked to see him in private one morning. They had the goods on him and Teel was fired immediately, owing the company more than $12,000!

While the company did not file embezzlement charges, they put a lien on Teel's car and house until he could repay all he had stolen. He felt so ashamed and guilty over what he had done, he almost couldn't face his wife and parents.

His hurt went extremely deep—so deep, he often couldn't sleep at night. With a wife who loved him, and parents who took care of the repayment, Teel eventually worked through his deep sense of hurt. In his words, however, "part of that pain will never go away."

THE HURT OF SEXUAL VIOLATION

Many people suffer in silence from being sexually molested as a child. The hurt never goes away. Most people have a way of "stuffing" that hurt, hiding it in the deep crevices of their souls so no one will know it's there. It too carries with it feelings of shame and disgrace.

Satan often uses memories of sexual violation to make the victim feel that it was her fault, instead of the fault of the perpetrator. Often the perpetrator said, "This is our little secret, so don't dare tell anyone about it." Even if not, victims of sexual abuse sometimes go many years without telling anyone what hurt and grief they've experienced. Rape victims often experience much the same degree of false guilt, shame, and emotional hurt.

COUNSEL FROM GOD'S WORD

No matter how you've been hurt in the past, God wants to heal your broken heart. Here's a step-by-step process that will bring deliverance.

1. First, forgive!

That's where it all begins. Holding a grudge or animosity against those who hurt you only blocks your own recovery. No matter what someone else has done:

> Be kind and compassionate to one another, forgiving each other,
> just as in Christ God forgave you (Ephesians 4:32).

Lack of forgiveness also blocks our prayers. Jesus taught this in the sermon on the mount:

> "For if you forgive men when they sin against you, your heavenly
> Father will also forgive you. But if you do not forgive men their
> sins, your Father will not forgive your sins" (Matthew 6:14-15).

The psalmist declared this same truth when he said: "If I had cherished sin in my heart, the Lord would not have listened" (Psalm 66:18).

When we ask anything from God, His answers are blocked if we're harboring ill will against someone else.

2. Hand your hurts over to God.

Like a traveler hands his luggage over to a skycap, you need to officially hand your hurts over to God.

The Bible says: "Cast all your anxiety on [the Lord] because he cares for you" (1 Peter 5:7). The word for "cast" in the original language means to decisively "throw".

That verse might be restated: "With all of your might, throw your cares, anxieties, burdens, and hurts on the Lord...."

Expressing the answer to many of the hurts he himself had suffered, Jeremiah Rankin wrote:

> Are you weary, are you heavy hearted? Tell it to Jesus, tell it to
> Jesus! Are you grieving over joys departed? Tell it to Jesus....

3. Share your hurts with someone who understands.

Contrary to popular opinion, God did not design us to fly solo through this life. We really do need each other. While Scripture tells us the Lord will sustain us, the Bible also teaches we need to confide in someone else in whom we can place our confidence.

The apostle Paul put it this way: "Carry each other's burdens, and in this way you will fulfill the law of Christ" (Galatians 6:2). For someone to help carry your hurts, however, he or she has to be told about your hurts.

Don't hold your hurts in. Instead, share them with someone you trust, someone who will pray for you and with you.

4. Begin praising the Lord daily.

You may ask, "But how can I praise God when I hurt so badly?" This is precisely when you need to praise Him!

Isaiah speaks of putting on a "garment of praise instead of a spirit of despair" (Isaiah 61:3). Praise has a way of releasing God's power and deliverance to us. Besides, the more we praise and worship God, the less we will be preoccupied with our own hurt.

No, this isn't whistling in the dark. It's following the divine pattern of Scripture. When Jonah began to praise God while in the belly of the fish, he was vomited out onto dry land. When Paul and Silas praised God while in jail, God brought an earthquake and opened the jail doors. Not only that, but the jailer and his family got saved in the process!

I would suggest you begin this praise process by praying through Psalms 95-150, the last part of the Bible's praise handbook.

5. Through prayer, allow God to use your hurt.

Jesus is our supreme example of effective prayer. He prayed often, not only fellowshipping with God though prayer, but also interceding for others (see John 17, for instance).

When the Lord allows hurt to come into your life, He wants not only to take that hurt away, but also to draw you closer to Himself as a result of all you've been through.

Sometimes people who have been deeply hurt find God has made them more sensitive to the needs of others, more patient, more tender. Hurt drives us to depend on the Lord, where otherwise we may not have.

That's why Paul said:

Indeed, in our hearts we felt the sentence of death. But this happened that we might not rely on ourselves but on God (2 Corinthian 1:9).

The apostle was referring to the hurt, the rejection, and the hardship he and other believers had experienced. In retrospect, he could see God was teaching him reliance and trust.

Sometimes the presence of hurt or disappointment is God's opportunity to do a miracle in our life. People who have gone through severe hurt are uniquely qualified to minister to others who hurt.

Remember Betty? She finally handed all of her hurts over to the Lord, then went to her husband and fully forgave him for all the damage he had done to her. He's changed, and she now feels free from the hurts of the past.

Though their marriage isn't perfect today, Betty and her husband are together and in love with each other.

God wants to heal the hurts in your life, too.

■ ■ ■ ■

More biblical counsel

PSALM 55:22

PSALM 56:3-4

PSALM 121

ZEPHANIAH 3:17-20

HABAKKUK 3:17-19

DEUTERONOMY 33:27

ACTS 3:1-10

MARK 10:46-52

HEBREWS 13:5B

2 CORINTHIANS 1:3-7

2 CORINTHIANS 3:4-6

Inferiority

Once you were not a people,
but now you are the people of God:
once you had not received mercy,
but now you have received mercy.

I PETER 2:10

■ ■ ■ ■ ■

I f I live to be one hundred, I'll never forget Faye. Quiet, somewhat shy, definitely melancholic, Faye constantly berated herself, telling herself and others that she was inept, lacked talent and finesse, and could never do anything right.

I later learned from Faye that her childhood was far from happy. Her parents divorced when Faye was only three, and her mother remarried three times. Of Faye's three step-fathers, two molested her while she was growing up. Just as devastating, her mother constantly put her down, and even told her on more than one occasion she wished Faye had never been born.

Faye was never congratulated or praised for her school work, and her chores at home were never completed well enough. Her mom criticized her relentlessly. Faye grew up with a very low opinion of herself. She feared trying anything new, and was horrified to assume any responsibility that might come under the scrutiny of someone else.

Faye felt so inferior to others it affected her ability to hold a job, go to college, or even get married. At thirty-eight years of age, she finally poured out her whole life to me, saying she felt like giving up.

Like Faye, many people suffer from deep feelings of inferiority. In Faye's words, they struggle with a deep "feeling of utter uselessness."

While the Bible warns against thinking of ourselves more highly than we ought (Romans 12:3), and commands us to look out not only for our own interests, but also for the interests of others (Philippians 2:4), nowhere in the Bible are we told to put down ourselves or wallow in our own failure.

CAUSES OF INFERIORITY FEELINGS

Before we outline God's cure, let's look at nine common causes of inferiority feelings.

1. Less than ideal physical stature and appearance.

Because of the inordinate emphasis placed on athletics, some young men are made to feel inferior by parents, coaches, and peers who place a high premium on excelling in competitive sports.

Because of our culture's insistence on equating thinness with beauty and success, many girls who are somewhat overweight also develop feelings of inferiority.

In addition, people with physical defects obvious for others to see tend to feel less than whole.

2. Academic limitations.

Most people are not straight-A students. Many don't fare well academically. That's not where their interests lie, yet they are constantly compared with those who do well in this area.

This often leads to feelings of inferiority.

In college, a friend of mine made fairly low scores on his exams. When grades came out, he had a way of disappearing while the rest of us compared scores. His grades often were one to two letters below the rest of us, causing deep feelings of inferiority.

3. Vocational and economical factors.

The kind of work one does and the amount of money one earns often prompt feelings of superiority or inferiority.

When I was a young boy, I had two good friends. One grew up to be a doctor, the other a handyman who repaired broken appliances in people's homes. For all the years I've known him, the repairman has had a deep feeling of inferiority, especially when he's around our doctor friend. Yet the services both men perform are equally necessary and important.

4. Negative comparisons made by one's parents.

Some people enter their adult years with inferior feelings because they were wrongfully compared with a sibling while growing up.

I know a family with two daughters. One daughter is Miss Extracurricular. She's into cheerleading, sports, music lessons, horseback riding, and is constantly running for an office in student government.

The other girl attends the same high school, but isn't into all those extracurricular activities. She's a very good student, but prefers domestic projects such as sewing or baking cookies.

The two sisters are total opposites, yet it's very easy to see the parents showing great partiality to their older daughter. They've even asked their younger daughter, "How come you don't go out for basketball, take piano lessons, or run for president of your class at school, like your sister?"

Clearly the parents don't realize what they are doing, creating seeds of deep-seated inferiority in that younger daughter.

5. Poor health.

People who find themselves in poor health much of their lives, with headaches, stomach disorders, skin rashes, or the like, tend to feel inferior.

As well, people who have gone through major surgery, have suffered the amputation of an arm or leg, are forced to wear a colostomy, have a brace, or are required to use a cane, crutches, or wheelchair, often look down on themselves.

6. Satanic oppression.

I'm convinced many people feel inferior, useless, and quite dispensable because Satan is oppressing them. If the devil can cause believers to lose sight of their identity in Christ and foist on them feelings of worthlessness, he can successfully keep them from serving God.

Much of the impetus Christians get for serving God is a sense of well-being in who they are in Christ. If we can be coaxed into believing the lie that we're somehow less than God says we are, we'll end up doing less than God says we can do, and accomplishing far less for the Kingdom than God says we can accomplish. It's that simple.

7. Criticism of others.

Like Faye, many people have been told by one or both parents that they are inferior, defective, and somehow don't measure up. Others have been harshly criticized by a teacher, coach, boss, or peer.

Since we have a propensity to become what we're told we are, it's no wonder some people develop deep feelings of inferiority.

If you find yourself constantly feeling inferior, whatever the reason might be, I urge you to take the following steps.

COUNSEL FROM GOD'S WORD

I. First, realize you're in good company!

Many Bible characters had feelings of inferiority.

Moses had a fantastic education, all the treasures of Egypt were once at his disposal, and he had the advantage of being raised in a family of notoriety. Yet later in life he felt inferior!

When God came to commission Moses, his response was: "Who am I, that I should go to Pharaoh and bring the Israelites out of Egypt?" (Exodus 3:11). He made the mistake of thinking God was asking him to deliver the Israelites from their bondage, when all God was asking him to be was the human instrument through which God Himself would deliver His people.

Moses also complained the Israelites wouldn't believe God has sent him. His self-esteem was so low, he feared any possibility of rejection or failure.

Jeremiah had a similar inferiority problem. When the call of God came to him, telling him he had been set apart to be a prophet, he responded: "Ah, Sovereign LORD...I do not know how to speak; I am only a child" (Jeremiah 1:6). The Lord finally had to tell Jeremiah not to worry about what to say, because He would put the words in his mouth. So often, our inferior feelings—like Jeremiah's—are baseless.

Amos was another great prophet who struggled with feelings of inferiority. A shepherd by trade, Amos was called by God to preach against the northern kingdom. The people there derided him, telling him to go on back home and preach against the sins of his own nation. In Amos 7:14, Amos responded that he was not a prophet, nor a prophet's son. He was feeling a little intimidated, having never been to prophet's school. Yet God used Amos anyway!

Elijah also suffered greatly from an inferiority complex. Totally intimidated by wicked queen Jezebel, he fled to a cave in the wilderness and cried out to the Lord in his despair:

> "The Israelites have rejected your covenant, broken down your
> altars, and put your prophets to death with a sword. I am the
> only one left, and now they are trying to kill me too" (1 Kings
> 19:10).

Just remember, all these men struggled with inferiority feelings, yet God used them in great ways.

2. Understand our sense of well-being isn't derived from what we have, but who we are in Christ.

The apostle Paul reminded the Corinthian believers:

> Brothers, think of what you were when you were called. Not
> many of you were wise by human standards; not many were
> influential; not many were of noble birth. But God chose the fool-
> ish things of the world to shame the wise; God chose the weak
> things of the world to shame the strong. He chose the lowly
> things of this world and the despised things—and the things that
> are not—to nullify the things that are, so that no one may boast
> before him (1 Corinthians 1:26-29).

By speaking of "foolish things," Paul is stressing the usability of all sorts of people. By "weak," Paul is showing God is not dependent on man's strength to accomplish His will. By "lowly," he's downplaying the importance of position. "Despised things" means things cursed by men—like the cross—which God uses for good. "Things that are not" refers to those persons or things which others consider non-entities.

It's not our pedigrees, prestige, friends, fame, income, or clout in life that give us a genuine sense of well-being. That only comes from knowing who we are in Christ.

Who are we? We're children of God (1 John 3:1). We're "heirs" of God and fellow heirs with Christ (Romans 8:17). We're "more than conquerors" (Romans 8:37). We're "the righteousness of God" (2 Corinthians 5:21). We're "new creatures" (2 Corinthians 5:17).

This doesn't mean we're to be lazy and lethargic! God wants our best and highest affection. In Matthew 22:37 we're told to "'Love the Lord your God with all of your heart and with all your soul and with all your mind.'" He wants all we have.

Someone has said: "It does not take much of a person to be a Christian, but it takes all of a person there is." How true, how true!

3. Remember, God uses ordinary people in extraordinary ways.

Abraham was an ordinary person, and so were Deborah, Ruth, David, Daniel, Esther, Nehemiah, John the Baptist, Peter, James, and John—yet look how God used them!

In Christian history, God also has used ordinary people like Corrie ten Boom, John Wycliffe, John Tyndale, John and Charles Wesley, D.L. Moody, Charles Finney, Charles Spurgeon, Fanny J. Crosby, Billy Graham, and many others in extraordinary ways.

Billy Sunday was uncouth in many ways. He played baseball for the Chicago White Stockings, then became a clerk at the YMCA, and only later became an evangelist. Totally unconventional, he broke chairs, did back flips, and often murdered the English language to make a point. Yet God used him to bring hundreds of thousands of people to Christ, including Billy Graham's father.

It's God's power—not man's credentials—that makes all the difference. When the religious authorities in Jesus' day saw what two men without credentials or political clout had accomplished, they were flabbergasted:

When they saw the courage of Peter and John, and realized that they were unschooled, ordinary men, they were astonished and they took note that these men had been with Jesus (Acts 4:13).

4. Remember, our goal is to please God, not man.

Most of our feelings of inferiority come from trying to measure up to other people's expectations and often falling short. The Bible makes it abundantly clear that our goal is to please the Lord.

The apostle Paul said: "We are not trying to please men but God, who tests our hearts" (1 Thessalonians 2:4b). On another occasion he wrote:

> Am I now trying to win the approval of men, or of God? Or am I trying to please men? If I were still trying to please men, I would not be a servant of Christ (Galatians 1:10).

5. Recognize that whatever we accomplish, we do so by God's strength.

When Israel's army couldn't defeat the giant Goliath with their sophisticated weaponry, the boy David dared challenge him:

> "You come against me with sword and spear and javelin, but I come against you in the name of the LORD Almighty, the God of the armies of Israel, whom you have defied" (1 Samuel 17:45).

When Peter and John were questioned concerning the healing of the man at the gate of the Temple, they made clear it wasn't their power at work:

> "If we are being called to account today for an act of kindness shown to a cripple, and are asked how he was healed, then know this, you and all the people of Israel: It is by the name of Jesus Christ of Nazareth, whom you crucified, but whom God raised from the dead, that this man stands before you healed" (Acts 4:9-10).

Paul could say, "I can do everything through him who gives me strength" (Philippians 4:13). Elsewhere, talking about how he went through several great trials, he wrote:

> Indeed, in our hearts we felt the sentence of death. But this hap-
> pened that we might not rely on ourselves but on God, who raises
> the dead (2 Corinthians 1:9).

God wants us to completely rely on Him for all things. Once we know that, we need never feel inferior again.

6. Let Christ live His life through you.

I used to think *I* had to do things for the Lord, until I learned what He really wants is to live His life through me.

Paul explained it this way: "I have been crucified with Christ and I no longer live, but Christ lives in me" (Galatians 2:20). Later he talked about "Christ in you, the hope of glory" (Colossians 1:27). He also wrote, "It is God who works in you to will and to act according to his good purpose" (Philippians 2:13).

Some people feel inferior, because they look around and see people apparently doing great and glorious things, not realizing whatever they are doing of eternal worth isn't being done *by* them, but by the Lord *through* them.

It's not me doing things for the Lord, but allowing Him to do His work in and through me.

This is why God reduced Gideon's army from 32,000 to three hundred, so when victory came, Gideon knew it was because of the Lord, not his own military prowess.

God doesn't use the best, just our best. That's all He asks. We're either "inhabited" by the Lord or "inhibited" without Him. It's up to us.

If you're in Christ, you're complete. You have it all. You have absolutely no reason to feel inferior, because "His divine power has given us everything we need for life and godliness" (2 Peter 1:3a). We're anything but inferior, no matter how inadequate we may feel compared to others.

What about Faye? She was greatly helped at a women's conference when she learned that her esteem and sufficiency were wrapped up in Christ and that she had all she needed to be what God wanted her to be. After that, she was able to walk with her head held high, realizing God was at work in and through her.

Remember, "nobody needs to be a nobody." In Christ, you're truly somebody!

■ ■ ■ ■ ■

More biblical counsel

GENESIS 1:27
PSALM 8:3-5
MATTHEW 6:27-30
EPHESIANS 2:10
1 CORINTHIANS 12:21-26
PSALM 139:13-16
ZEPHANIAH 3:17
1 PETER 2:9-10
REVELATION 20:6
PSALM 63:3
PSALM 86:13
JEREMIAH 31:3
EPHESIANS 1:1-10
1 CORINTHIANS 15:10A

Lust

*Therefore do not let sin
reign in your mortal body so
that you obey its evil desires.*

ROMANS 6:12

■ ■ ■ ■ ■

When I met Andre, he had known the Lord for only about six months. He fidgeted with a piece of paper for a few minutes, then looked me in the eye. "I may as well get right to the issue," he said nervously. "I have an uncontrollable sexual urge, and I need help."

It didn't help that Andre was handsome. He was fairly tall and muscular, with dark hair and dark eyes. He also had an outgoing personality. He had been out of college only a year; while there, he had sowed wild oats, getting hooked on sex.

Andre admitted: "I can't stop thinking about women. I fantasize and dream about them constantly."

When he accepted Christ, Andre thought his problem would automatically disappear. It didn't, and he was now in a state of panic. Feeling guilty and disgusted with himself, Andre had come for some answers.

America is full of Andres. Our society has gone through a sexual revolution the past three decades. The porn industry now grosses billions every year. Nearly all standards have been torn down. Men like Andre see sex in advertising, on television, in newspapers, on billboards, and hear about it in abundance on the radio. We're a sex-saturated culture.

God created sex, but set limits for its enjoyment. To experience sex outside the boundary lines of marriage is to pervert something very sacred into something very cheap and selfish.

DO CHRISTIANS STRUGGLE WITH LUST?

When we were saved by Jesus Christ, we died to sin (Romans 6:2). The old nature in us came to an end. That doesn't mean the struggle is over, however, since sin still operates in the sphere of our physical bodies and minds. But sin doesn't have the upper hand anymore, if we're in Christ.

Today, therapists and counselors refer to sexual "addiction." It's a new term, but an old problem. Jesus talked about it in His sermon on the mount:

> "You have heard that it was said, 'Do not commit adultery.' But I tell you that anyone who looks at a woman lustfully has already committed adultery with her in his heart" (Matthew 5:27).

Jesus made it absolutely clear that sexual lust begins in the eye, then moves quickly to the heart. Perhaps this is why Job wrote: "I made a covenant with my eyes not to look lustfully at a girl" (Job 31:1).

So the answer is yes, you will struggle with sexual lust as a Christian unless you take some precautions to keep it in check.

Jesus said that temptation to sin is sure to come. Lust is one of the most common temptations. The key is what we do with lust when it tempts us.

HOW DO I KNOW IF I HAVE A LUST PROBLEM?

After answering this series of questions, you'll be able to discern whether or not you are a victim of lust.

- Do I find myself thinking about sex (with someone other than my spouse) a good deal of the time?
- Do I even occasionally view pornography, either in print or in videos?
- Do I find myself talking about sex a lot (with someone other than my spouse)?
- Do I find myself mentally "undressing" people of the opposite sex when I look at them?

- Do I have trouble concentrating on any one thing except sex for very long?
- Do I have dreams from time to time about sexual escapades?
- Do I have a propensity to touch people of the opposite sex when greeting them or talking to them?
- Do I ever find myself "planning" for lust?

If your answer to most of those questions is "yes," you have a lust problem. Of course, not everybody who struggles with sexual compulsions is an addict.

COUNSEL FROM GOD'S WORD

If you and I don't gain and maintain victory over lust, we'll struggle in every other area of life. The following sequential steps will enable you to gain victory in this difficult area.

1. Recognize the source of all lust.

Does lust just drop out from the sky? Do we inherit the propensity for lust from our forefathers? Is it simply part of our make-up, temperament, or nationality? Where does it come from?

Jesus taught us the source of sexual lust is the heart:

"What comes out of a man is what makes him 'unclean.' For from within, out of men's hearts, come evil thoughts, sexual immorality, theft, murder, adultery, greed, malice, deceit, lewdness, envy, slander, arrogance and folly. All these evils come from inside and make a man unclean" (Mark 7:20-23).

Jesus put His finger on the source. Lust springs from what Paul called the "body of sin." It's from within, triggered by what is without. But it all begins in the mind. We don't have to guess who places it there. Satan would love nothing better than to see your mind totally infected with filth, lewdness, and insatiable lust.

In the arena of the mind we either resist or give into temptation. James tells us in his epistle that

... .each one is tempted when by his own evil desire he is dragged
away and enticed. Then, after desire has conceived, it gives birth
to sin, and sin when it is full grown, gives birth to death (James
1:14-15).

The cycle always progresses from the mind to "death," without exception,
unless we cry out to God for help.

2. Quit rationalizing and confess lust as sin.

It's amazing how our culture has relabeled certain sins so they don't
sound so bad anymore. We call fornication "co-habitation." We call homosexuality "an alternative life-style."

Like any other sin, lust can be rationalized, relabeled...or confessed. God's
solution is confession. Solomon wrote, "He who conceals his sins does not
prosper" (Proverbs 28:13). As long as we try to hide our lust problem, we'll
never break its stranglehold.

It's amazing how when a horrible sex crime is committed against a
woman or child, the public says of the offender: "He's really *sick* to do something like that." Popular psychology explains away peoples' terrible actions as
symptoms of an ill-defined disease, completely removing such actions from the
realm of morality.

The Lord doesn't want us rationalizing sin away by saying, "We all have
certain weaknesses. This just happens to be mine." That's denying the serious-
ness of lust, cutting ourselves off from God's remedy.

The Bible is clear that lust is a *moral* issue:

Do not love the world, or anything in the world. If anyone loves
the world, love of the Father is not in him. For everything in the
world—the cravings of sinful man, the lust of his eyes and the
boasting of what he has and does—comes not from the Father
but from the world (1 John 2:15-16).

What the New International Version calls "the cravings of sinful man"
older Bible versions refer to as "the lust of the flesh." One thing is clear: it is sin,

and sin needs to be confessed! First John 1:9 promises us that if we will confess our sins, God *will* forgive us.

3. Also, confess your lust to a trusted friend of the same sex.

In James 5:16, we're told to confess our sins to each other. This not only brings accountability, but also encouragement. The Bible tells us: "Therefore encourage one another and build each other up, just as in fact you are doing" (1 Thessalonians 5:11).

As in any other area of life, we need someone who will dare to ask us the hard questions. A mature Christian brother or sister who loves us will be willing to do just that for our deliverance.

Make sure the friend you pick is trustworthy. Nothing is accomplished by putting our dirty laundry on the public line.

4. Understand God wills for you to be pure.

Many people are anxious to know God's will. But God's Word makes known His will in every vital area of life. This area is no exception:

> It is God's will that you should be sanctified: that you should
> avoid sexual immorality; that each of you should learn to control
> his own body in a way that is holy and honorable, not in passion-
> ate lust like the heathen, who do not know God; and that in this
> matter no one should wrong his brother or take advantage of
> him. The Lord will punish men for all such sins, as we have
> already told you and warned you. For God did not call us to be
> impure, but to live a holy life. Therefore he who rejects this
> instruction does not reject man, but God (1 Thessalonians 4:3-8).

As Christians, we have *positional* holiness. Christ's righteousness was imputed to us the moment we received Him. But *practical* holiness comes as we allow God to work out of us in daily living that which He already has worked into us.

5. Avoid convenient reminders.

Since outward stimuli serve as footholds for Satan to defeat us, we need to avoid them like the plague! The Bible says we're to avoid "every kind of evil" (1 Thessalonians 5:22). We have a divine obligation to keep our eyes off anything and everything that would trigger lust within us.

In 2 Samuel 11, King David fell into immorality because he didn't guard his eyes. Someone described the process this way: he looked, he lusted, he leaped, he laid, then he lied to cover up. The consequences were devastating.

If eating is your weakness, don't visit the local donut shop! If new cars are your weakness, don't visit an auto dealership for another three or four years. If stealing is your problem, don't go in stores alone. If drinking alcohol is your weakness, don't drive by the tavern on the way home. If lust is your problem, don't look at that which will provoke you to lust.

6. Experience daily cleansing of the mind.

Since we lose or win every battle in the mind, Scripture tells us to have the mind of Jesus (Philippians 2:5). We're also commanded to set our hearts (minds) on the things above (Colossians 3:2).

If lust is a problem, God urges you to "be made new in the attitude of your minds" (Ephesians 4:23). Daily renewal can only come about as we get into God's Word consistently. "How can a young man keep his way pure?" the psalmist asks. "By living according to your word" (Psalm 119:9). The power of the Word has a cleansing and prompting effect nothing else can match.

I challenge you to spend as much quantity time in God's Word as you do eating each day. The care and feeding of your soul is vitally important!

7. Put on the armor of God and pray daily for His protection.

The New Testament urges us to put on the armor of God, which includes the belt of truth, the breastplate of righteousness, the shoes of the gospel of peace, the shield of faith, the helmet of salvation, and the sword of the Spirit, which is the Word of God.

Paul then goes on to urge us to "pray in the Spirit at all times" (Ephesians 6:18). This is praying with complete trust that the Holy Spirit will present our prayers to God the Father in just the right way (Romans 8:26).

Why pray to God when temptation comes? So that "you may be able to stand your ground" (Ephesians 6:13).

You may wonder what happened to Andre. He finally surrendered his life over the Lordship of Christ, and was discipled by an older man for almost a year. Andre overcame the lust problem in his life. He is still tempted, of course, but by applying the seven steps described above he's learned how to ward off temptation.

If you're struggling with lust, cry out to God right now: Lord, cleanse me! Scape the barnacles of lust and filth from my mind. Wash me clean of all the debris and filth of a dirty world, so that my fellowship with You will be undefiled. I hereby totally surrender my mind and eyes to You, and ask for a hedge of purity to surround my being. In Jesus' name, Amen.

• • • • •

More biblical counsel

I CORINTHIANS 6:13
ISAIAH 55:7
ISAIAH 1:16-18
ROMANS 13:14
TITUS 2:11-12
PSALM 51
PSALM 32
I PETER 1:14-16
GALATIANS 5:16-23
PROVERBS 6:25
PROVERBS 5:15-23
I CORINTHIANS 7
2 CORINTHIANS 6:14-18

Lying

Therefore each of you must put off falsehood
and speak truthfully to his neighbor,
for we are all members of one body.
EPHESIANS 4:25

■ ■ ■ ■ ■

To conceal her identity, I'll call her Ann. She was an attractive woman in her mid-thirties, with a career in real estate. Professionally, she was very successful, and was certainly known by her peers in commercial real estate as a "female tycoon." She was responsible for closing some of the largest and most profitable real estate deals in our city, and her picture often appeared in the business section of our leading newspaper.

In addition to being successful, Ann was married to a medical student in his last year of internship before going into private practice. Both were church-goers, and outwardly appeared to be a couple on their way to the top.

But what was concealed suddenly became revealed. Ann had a serious problem with telling the truth, not only in her business world, but at home, church, and wherever else her presence was made known.

When caught in a lie, Ann would say there must have been a lack of communication, or would profusely apologize and say that she didn't really think she said that, but if she did she was sorry.

It worked most of the time. Her husband—we'll call him Ed—came to me when Ann began lying about her schedule, especially her late nights, which were increasing in number.

Ed suspected she was seeing another man, but certainly couldn't prove it. He had learned to tell when Ann was lying, however, and when she wasn't. The big day of confrontation came as they both sat in my office and I lovingly confronted Ann with her problem of lying in general, and lying about her schedule in particular. Her response? We'll see later.

Ann's case is not isolated. Whether in the business, sports, or entertainment world, or in the home, lying is on the increase. Lying in government also is epidemic, and it is now estimated that as many as 44 percent of all college students lie (cheat) to pass their exams.

WHY DO PEOPLE LIE HABITUALLY?

Modern psychology refers to people who habitually lie as pathological liars, suggesting they're abnormally conditioned to lie about almost anything. It's sometimes said that such deviant behavior stems to a particular childhood event or series of events, and that it will take a great deal of therapy to break someone of the habit.

In getting to the root cause of lying, various explanations and theories abound. On the surface, however, why do people lie?

1. To get their own way.

Christian psychologist David Ritzenthaler suggests most people lie to manipulate situations in an effort to get other people to do what they want them to do. They also lie to get relationships to work the way they want them to work, although this seldom ultimately happens.

Why else do people habitually lie?

2. Feelings of Inferiority.

Some people lie because they have a deep sense of inadequacy. Such individuals don't excel at many things so, to save face, they lie. A teenager who isn't great at athletics may make up a story about an ache or pain to justify the baskets he missed or the times he struck out. Lying makes him feel accepted, even praised for skills he really doesn't have.

3. Some lie to be accepted by others.

Peer pressure is strong, so some people lie in order to be one of the bunch, to be accepted by all. A teenage girl may boast about the number of dates she's had with guys when she's in a group of girls boasting about all the dates they have gone on. This way, she avoids embarrassment in front of and possible rejection from her peers. Because lying gives some a false feeling of importance, success, and even authority, they adjust the facts to make themselves look good.

4. Some lie to avoid consequences.

Children lie to avoid a spanking. Teenagers lie to avoid being grounded. Students lie so they won't flunk a course. Employees lie so they won't be fired. Politicians lie so they won't lose an election. Athletes lie to keep from getting kicked off the team. Spouses lie to keep their marriages from falling apart. Some lie to keep from going to jail.

5. Some lie to maintain an image they want to project to others.

Sales people may lie about their product to make it appear superior to other brands. Neighbors may lie about their income to other neighbors to maintain a successful image. Men will often lie to each other about their sexual conquests to maintain a macho image. A husband may lie to his wife to keep her thinking he's a family man, when in fact he's having an affair on the side. Many business owners will lie about their businesses in order to project an image of success so others will buy more from them.

6. Some lie for material gain alone.

Much lying in America is materialistic in nature. Some make claims for their product that cannot be substantiated. Salesmen and others who frequently travel may lie about their expense accounts, often padding them significantly. People lie by failing to report income to the Internal Revenue Service.

As I write these lines, a popular television personality in our area who runs hundreds of ads weekly touting his ability to help individuals quit smoking, was just ordered by the state attorney general to cease and desist his ads because they are deceptive. Why? Because his ads imply that the people quit smoking, when in fact they may quit smoking only for the duration of his seminar.

7. They have become duplicitous.

Lying has become a way of life for many. They fall into the subtle trap of not only having no conscience about lying, but actually not being aware at the time that they're telling a lie.

TYPES OF LYING

There are many kinds of lying.

Lying can take on the form of withholding the truth, not giving all the facts. When someone sells a used car and knows something is wrong with it, but fails to inform the buyer, he's lying. The seller has deceived the buyer.

Not informing the consumer of the fine print is a form of lying.

When a wife asks her husband, "Where have you been all night?" and he responds, "At the office, buried all night," when in fact he's been buried on the couch with the office secretary, he's lying to his wife.

Flattery is another form of lying. Passing on exaggerated compliments to others to curry favor is lying.

There is also exaggeration. Saying, "There were hundreds present for the concert," when 168 showed up, is a form of lying. "It's the number one vacuum cleaner in the USA." That statement, when not backed up by sales figures, can be deceiving, and thus is a form of lying.

Other people gloss over details, hoping people won't ask about them specific questions, and this too is a form of lying.

COUNSEL FROM GOD'S WORD

If you have a problem with not always telling the truth, or if you're prone to exaggerate, here's a step-by-step path to victory.

I. Acknowledge that lying is wrong—it's a serious spiritual problem.

Behavioral sciences like sociology and psychology can study lying all they want, but lying is still a sin and needs to be dealt with biblically.

When Solomon listed what God hates most of all, guess what nearly topped the list?

There are six things the Lord hates, seven that are detestable to him: haughty eyes, a lying tongue... (Proverbs 6:16-17).

God hates lying. In that same list, Solomon adds that God hates "a false witness who pours out lies" (Proverbs 6:19).

As pertains to the business world, Solomon says: "The wicked man earns deceptive wages" (Proverbs 11:18). And again: "The Lord detests lying lips, but he delights in men who are truthful" (Proverbs 12:22).

Solomon further says: "Arrogant lips are unsuited to a fool—how much worse lying lips to a ruler" (Proverbs 17:7).

In the New Testament, we're given strict orders as Christians: "Do not lie to each other, since you have taken off your old self with its practices" (Colossians 3:9).

2. Understand that lying has grave consequences.

Since many lies are eventually brought to light, we need to be keenly aware that lying today brings disaster tomorrow. We always reap what we sow.

Again, we're warned in Proverbs about the consequences of lying: "A man of perverse heart does not prosper; he whose tongue is deceitful falls into trouble" (Proverbs 17:20). And, "A false witness will not go unpunished, and he who pours out lies will perish" (Proverbs 19:9).

Solomon gives an even more grave warning when he says: "A fortune made by a lying tongue is a fleeting vapor and a deadly snare" (Proverbs 21:6).

In referring to a dishonest court system, Solomon says: "Whoever says to the guilty, 'You are innocent'—peoples will curse him and nations denounce him" (Proverbs 24:24).

And again about government: "If a ruler listens to lies, all his officials become wicked" (Proverbs 29:12).

Perhaps the most sobering warning of all is given in Acts 5. When Annanias and Sapphira lied about their gift to the church, they both died on the spot. God absolutely hates lying.

3. Remember, if you lie, you hate the one to whom you lie.

Lying hurts the one who is lied to, not just the liar. Solomon warns: "A lying tongue hates those it hurts, and a flattering mouth works ruin" (Proverbs 26:28).

Nowhere is this more true than in the marriage relationship. This is why no marriage can survive long if one or both spouses practice lying.

4. Repent of lying, and acknowledge to God it is sin.

The apostle Paul says:

Godly sorrow brings repentance that leads to salvation and leaves no regret, but worldly sorrow brings death (2 Corinthians 7:10).

We need to express contrition that we have violated the truth, and in a sense violated other people by deceiving them. When possible, we need to go to the people to whom we've lied or exaggerated, and ask their forgiveness, telling them the truth.

When you confess this sin to God, ask for His forgiveness (1 John 1:9). Don't try to justify to God or others what you have done. Remember, "he who conceals his sins does not prosper" (Proverbs 28:13).

The consequences of coming clean and acknowledging you've lied are minimal compared to the consequences of continuing your lying. Two verses are particularly sobering. First, in Paul's list of those who won't inherit the kingdom of God, he lists "swindlers" (1 Corinthians 6:10). Revelation also makes it clear:

But the cowardly, the unbelieving, the vile, the murderers, the sexually immoral, those who practice magic arts, the idolaters, and all liars—their place will be in the fiery lake of burning sulfur. This is the second death (Revelation 21:8).

Real repentance and confession of sin are honored by God, who will give you the power to put away all lying forever.

5. Find a good friend who will hold you accountable.

Of course we're accountable to God, but in addition, we need a Paul who will hold our feet to the fire, and have the courage to ask us the hard questions. Remember, we're told in James 5:16 to confess our sins to one another and pray for one another. I believe this includes accountability.

If we don't ask someone we respect and love to hold us accountable, we're probably not serious about desiring to be free from lying.

6. Realize that you don't have to lie to be effective, respected, and greatly used by God.

God wants you to be yourself. His message needs no exaggeration or alteration. That's why we're told in Ephesians 4:15 to speak the truth in love.

Jesus said in the sermon on the mount that our words to others shouldn't be embellished:

> "Simply let your 'Yes' be 'Yes,' and your 'No,' 'No'; anything
> beyond this comes from the evil one" (Matthew 5:37).

We cannot, by lying, control what others think of us. Nor can we increase the respect of others by giving them a false impression of us.

You may have wondered what Ann's response was to the confrontation. First of all, her husband and I learned that no one in her whole life had ever confronted her lying and exaggerations. So her initial reaction was one of anger as she took on a martyr's spirit.

But after a few minutes had passed with a lot of tears, Ann broke down and told us that she had a problem with lying since she was a little girl in grade school, trying to explain to the other children why her clothes were hand-me-downs instead of new.

When Ann saw that lying put her in better graces with her peers, she continued throughout high school lying about how much her father made, when in reality her father abandoned her mother when she was only a baby. Her lying became a pattern to "help" her climb the ladder of success in her real estate business.

But now she was tired of lying to cover up past lies, and openly acknowledged everything, including the beginnings of an affair. A small group of women in our church met with Ann regularly, once she said she wanted to be free from the spirit of a lying tongue.

I'm happy to report that Ann gained victory over this sin and is a changed woman. Her marriage is intact, and her career is going better than ever, built upon the truth.

■ ■ ■ ■ ■

More biblical counsel

ROMANS 9:1

1 CORINTHIANS 13:6

EPHESIANS 6:14

1 TIMOTHY 2:7

2 TIMOTHY 3:8

2 TIMOTHY 4:4

TITUS 1:1

TITUS 1:14

EPHESIANS 4:15

1 PETER 1:22

1 JOHN 1:6

1 JOHN 1:8

1 JOHN 2:4

1 JOHN 2:21

2 CORINTHIANS 6:7

PROVERBS 6:14-19

PROVERBS 11:18

PROVERBS 12:19-20

PROVERBS 14:5

PROVERBS 14:25

PROVERBS 19:22

Marital Difficulties

*Make sure that nobody pays back
wrong for wrong, but always try to be
kind to each other and to everyone else.*

1 THESSALONIANS 5:15

■ ■ ■ ■ ■

Derald and Kim could easily have been voted an all-American, all-Christian couple. Into their marriage almost eight years, both were thirty years old, with two preschool children. Kim was quite active at church, ministering in both the nursery and preschool areas. Derald wasn't as active, but was always on call when we needed guys for a work party.

No one would have ever guessed they had any marital problems until a letter came from Kim revealing their marriage was a hollow facade. They were very close to separation. Derald showed virtually no affection to her once they were out of public view, except when he wanted sex.

Kim's reaction to Derald's emotional coolness was one of cynicism and defeatism. It became a vicious cycle. His lack of interest and affection greatly dulled her interest, which created yet even greater disinterest on his part. They were on a no-win merry-go-round headed for despair and destruction. Only Kim and Derald's very best friends knew the severity of the situation.

Marriage is in severe trouble today. A frightening number of people are now postponing marriage or avoiding it altogether until they're in their late thirties or early forties. The percentage of single people in our country today has never been higher.

Another disturbing trend is this: while it is said 50 percent of all new first-time marriages end in divorce within an average of seven years, it's reported a whopping 65 percent of spouses view their intact marriages as unfulfilling and dissatisfying.

While most marriage problems develop out of a failure to fulfill one's gender role in marriage, failure in several other major areas also cause marriage to be less than blissful.

PARENTAL CONFLICT

While not the major source of marital conflict, poor parental relationships can damage a marriage. Perhaps the biggest area of tension is where one spouse cannot cut the emotional umbilical cord from his or her parents.

Sadly, many parents don't encourage their grown, married children to be independent, but instead keep the door open for their son or daughter to run back to them with every problem or challenge he or she encounters.

Of course, every parent wants to "be there" for his or her child. But moms and dads must realize it's possible to be there too much of the time. From the beginning, God has said:

For this reason a man will leave his father and mother and be
united to his wife, and they will become one flesh (Genesis 2:24).

Jesus quoted this same verse in Matthew 19, and the apostle Paul quoted it in Ephesians 5. God's trying to tell us something! Parents can be a wonderful source of counsel and encouragement, especially in the early months of marriage. After all, the Bible tells us that: "parents are the pride of their children" (Proverbs 17:6).

There is a fine line between being helpful, however, and starting to interfere. Derald and Kim were having great difficulty because she was extremely close to her mom and on more than one occasion teamed up with her mom against Derald.

SEXUAL PROBLEMS

Both men and women have sexual needs, but the way to fulfill those needs varies from spouse to spouse. Most men don't realize that sex begins actually in the kitchen where he compliments his wife on the meal and gives her a kiss. It continues when he's willing to turn off the television to communicate with her. It continues as they go to bed, where he holds his wife and spends plenty of time with her before engaging in sex. It takes a woman far longer to be sexually satisfied than it does a man, and sensitivity needs to be the key here.

In most cases, a husband wants sex far more frequently than his wife. He is into the physical part of sex, while his wife is into the emotional and physical aspects. Some men are not willing to wait, but the wise husband will take all the time necessary.

On the other hand, a woman needs to realize the incredibly high sex drive her husband may have, and be willing to meet his needs.

Scripture addresses both husband and wife:

The husband should fulfill his marital duty to his wife, and likewise the wife to her husband. The wife's body does not belong to her alone, but also to her husband. In the same way the husband's body does not belong to him alone but also his wife (1 Corinthians 7:3-4).

We're called to meet each others' sexual needs, not just concentrate on our own needs. Paul goes on in that same chapter to say:

Do not deprive each other except by mutual consent and for a time, so that you may devote yourself to prayer (1 Corinthians 7:5).

In other words, we may have a lot of rights in marriage, but one of them is definitely not to withhold sex from our partner.

A good section of Scripture to concentrate on if you're going through problems in this area is found in the last chapter of Proverbs:

A wife of noble character who can find? She is worth far more than rubies. Her husband has full confidence in her and lacks nothing of value. She brings him good, not harm, all the days of his life (Proverbs 31:10-12).

FINANCIAL PROBLEMS

These problems develop quickly if a man and woman enter into marriage with wrong expectations. A wife raised in an affluent home may have a hard time adjusting to not going out and buying a dress, coat, or shoes whenever she wants them. A husband who spent money foolishly prior to marriage may find some conflict when he attempts to do the same after, especially when he's married to a woman who believes in budgeting every nickel.

The best way to solve this problem is to develop a Christian understanding of the biblical view of money. That view includes the fact that God owns everything (Psalm 24:1). We are simply stewards of what He owns (Matthew 25:14-30). God expects us to return to Him a tenth of all that comes to us (Malachi 3:9-11). God provides us with more than enough to give when we give to Him first (Proverbs 3:9-10, Luke 6:38, Ecclesiastes 11:1-2).

The other way to alleviate financial differences is to have an agreed upon budget and stick with it except in case of emergency. This applies to every dollar you have to spend, no matter how little or how much you make.

COMMUNICATION PROBLEMS

Lack of good, clear, and upbuilding communication in marriage is almost epidemic. Good lines of communication must be diligently maintained if a marriage is to succeed.

Many women wish their husbands would talk more, communicate more, and express their true feelings. Because that doesn't come naturally for most men, they have to work at it.

A good piece of advice to every married couple is found in these words penned by the apostle Paul:

Let your conversation be always full of grace, seasoned with salt
so that you may know how to answer everyone (Colossians 4:6).

There are all kinds of words—blaming words, critical words, sarcastic words, complaining words, condemning words. But marriage, of all places, deserves kind and compassionate words. Few things wound more deeply than verbal abuse. One woman told me she would have rather suffered physical abuse than verbal abuse. It can permanently damage a relationship.

Solomon observed: "A gentle answer turns away wrath" (Proverbs 15:1), but "A fool's mouth is his undoing" (Proverbs 18:7). He also noted: "The tongue has the power of life and death" (Proverbs 18:21).

Jesus showed how important words are when He said: "For by your words you will be acquitted, and by your words you will be condemned" (Matthew 12:37).

Don't underestimate the power of the tongue to harass, to put down, and to damage severely a lovely relationship. There is no place in marriage for communication that is less than loving and kind.

MUTUAL RESPECT

Many otherwise good relationships erode if this is lost. The Bible makes it abundantly clear that we must have—and show—respect for our spouses.

In his famous passage on marriage, Paul says: "Each one of you also must love his wife as he loves himself, and the wife must respect her husband" (Ephesians 5:33).

In his first epistle, Peter commands husbands to do the same:

Husbands, in the same way, be considerate as you live with your
wives, and treat them with respect. . . (1 Peter 3:7).

If you don't respect your spouse, you open the door for Satan to inflict great damage in your marriage. Respect means treating your spouse better than you treat your boss, parents, neighbors, or anyone else who deserves your best.

Apart from Jesus Christ, the person you ought to respect and esteem most is your spouse.

LACK OF FORGIVENESS

Perhaps the greatest problem in many marriages today is a reluctance or refusal to forgive when there's been an offense. Cliff Barrows says there are ten words that will safeguard a marriage: "I was wrong," "I'm sorry," "Forgive me," and "I love you!"

The Bible makes it clear we're not to go to bed while carrying a grudge: "Do not let the sun go down while you are still angry, and do not give the devil a foothold" (Ephesians 4:26b-27).

This is another way of saying, "Clear the slate daily." Don't let grudges and grievances carry over.

In that same chapter, Paul goes on to say:

Be kind and compassionate to one another, forgiving each other,
just as in Christ God forgave you (Ephesians 4:32).

We have an obligation, especially in the marriage relationship, to keep short accounts and readily forgive, just as the Lord has forgiven us.

Most marriages problems can be solved in large part if this principle is put into practice, and both husband and wife commit to truly loving each other.

COUNSEL FROM GOD'S WORD

Whatever your underlying problem, here are ten key biblical principles to apply to your marriage.

1. Make Jesus Christ first in your marriage (Matthew 6:33).

Be sure every decision you make honors Him.

2. Attend church weekly as a couple (Hebrews 10:25).

Don't let anything stop you from worship. The couple that worships God and serves Him together will not soon be torn apart from each other.

3. Concentrate on your role in marriage (Ephesians 5:21-33).

If you're a man, make sure you love your wife as Christ loves the church. If you're the woman, make sure you respect your husband as the head of your marriage, even if you feel he's not always the man you want him to be.

4. Make sure your words to each other are kind and considerate.

Say nothing you'll have to apologize for later (Proverbs 12:25, 13:3, 25:11, 26:28, 29:20).

5. Pray daily for each other.

Pray together as often as you can (Ephesians 6:18, Philippians 4:6, Matthew 18:19).

6. Focus on meeting each other's needs.

Do so rather than demanding that your own needs are met (Philippians 2:3-4).

7. Learn to be patient with each other.

Don't try to remake your spouse (1 Thessalonians 5:14).

8. Never try to get back at your spouse (1 Thessalonians 5:15, Romans 12:17).

9. Decide to make the Lord first in your finances (2 Corinthians 9:6-11).

10. Never consider divorce an option (1 Corinthians 7:10-11).

Remember, your marriage is a covenant God says cannot be broken.

You may be wondering about Derald and Kim. I'm glad to report that in their case, Derald learned what it means to love your wife as Christ loved the church, and Kim learned what it means to love her husband. Separation and potential divorce were diverted, but not until both of them allowed Jesus to be the Lord of their lives.

■ ■ ■ ■ ■

More biblical counsel

GENESIS 2-3

MALACHI 2:13-16

COLOSSIANS 3:18-19

COLOSSIANS 3:12-14

1 CORINTHIANS 13

MATTHEW 6:14-15

JAMES 4:10

1 CORINTHIANS 15:58

PROVERBS 18:13

PROVERBS 18:19

ECCLESIASTES 5:2-3

PROVERBS 13:3

Occult

He who does what is sinful is
of the devil, because the devil
has been sinning from the beginning.
The reason the Son of God appeared
was to destroy the devil's work.

I JOHN 3:8

■ ■ ■ ■ ■

Occultism is probably the fastest growing religion in our country today. It's revival can be mostly attributed to the New Age movement, touted widely by such visible celebrities as Shirley McClaine and John Denver.

While participation in the occult may range from casually reading one's horoscope in the daily newspaper to overt witchcraft and devil worship, the occult and its horrible effects have touched almost every family in America.

I'll call him Ted to conceal his real identity. I first met Ted when Rich, another young man who's a member of our church, made an appointment for me to see the two of them. Rich warned me that Ted had been dabbling with the ouija board, tarot cards, crystals, and séances.

Since they shared an apartment, Rich at first became very concerned and finally issued an edict. Either Ted had to get rid of all the books and magazines in their apartment that dealt with the occult, or he would have to move out. Ted agreed to get rid of the stuff, and also said he needed help getting the stuff out of his mind.

Rich felt Ted needed to be counseled and prayed over by me, and further asked me to dispose of Ted's books, tapes, and other paraphernalia related to the world of spirits.

Both young men came into my office carrying large grocery bags of occult materials. Instantly, a horrible odor began to emit from the bags. It became so toxic, we had to place the bags outside my back office door. (It took about an hour for the putrid odor to dissipate. I'd never smelled anything like it before.) Then our prayer meeting began.

Most people who get hooked on the occult do so gradually and somewhat innocently—reading the horoscope, celebrating Halloween, going through a "haunted" house, reading and putting stock in fortune cookie messages, being hypnotized, or having one's palm read. Increased involvement in the occult is oppressive, habit-forming, and highly destructive.

COMMON OCCULTIC PRACTICES

1. Spiritism

This is the belief that individuals can allegedly make contact with the dead through a medium in order to receive revelations from the spirit world.

One of the oldest events of this on record is when King Saul disguised himself, went to the witch of Endor, and requested that she bring up the prophet Samuel.

2. Clairvoyance

This is the belief that certain people possess the extrasensory ability to perceive what ordinarily cannot be seen. Most fortune tellers claim to have the spirit of clairvoyance.

3. Fortune telling

This is the practice of people who claim clairvoyant powers, and thus who allegedly can predict future events in people's lives. This is often done by reading palms, using tarot cards, or interpreting tea leaves (an ancient Babylonian pagan rite).

4. Astrology

This is the belief that the future can be foretold by studying the relative positions of the sun, moon, stars, and planets. Astrologers claim to be able to predict the destiny of even governments and nations by interpreting the alignment of certain stars and planets in the solar system.

5. Horoscopes

Belief in horoscopes is an outgrowth of astrology. Horoscopes purport to tell people what to watch for and how to behave, based on their date of birth, which is correlated to one of the signs of the zodiac.

6. Witchcraft

This false and often demon-inspired religious system has its roots in ancient pagan practices. It goes back before the time of the Babylonian and Egyptian empires, when priests and priestesses practiced occultic rituals and chants. Witches often allege they are able to contact and utilize powers from the unseen world.

7. Channeling

This recently revived practice calls for certain "gifted" individuals to go into a trance, during which time they are purportedly overtaken by an ancient spirit, who speaks through them.

IS THE OCCULT WRONG IN GOD'S EYES?

Through the story of King Saul's visit to the witch of Endor, Scripture makes clear what God thought about that practice:

> Saul died because he was unfaithful to the Lord; he did not keep
> the word of the Lord and even consulted a medium for guidance,
> and did not inquire of the Lord. So the Lord put him to death
> and turned the kingdom over to David son of Jesse (1 Chronicles
> 10:13-14).

King Saul was without excuse. He knew exactly what God has said from earliest times:

> Let no one be found among you...who practices divination or sorcery, interprets omens, engages in witchcraft, or casts spells, or who is a medium or spiritist or who consults the dead. Anyone who does these things is detestable to the Lord (Deuteronomy 18:10-12).

Turning back just a page, Scripture also is very clear what God thinks of astrology:

> If a man or woman living among you in one of the towns the Lord gives you is found doing evil in the eyes of the Lord your God in violation of his covenant, and contrary to my command has worshiped other gods, bowing down to them or to the sun or the moon or the stars of the sky, and this has been brought to your attention, then you must investigate it thoroughly. If it is true...take the man or woman who has done this evil deed to your city gate, and stone that person to death (Deuteronomy 17:2-5).

In Isaiah 47:11-15, a long list of evil practices are mentioned, including casting magic spells, sorceries, astrology, stargazing, and fortune-telling.

The list of those who will be thrown into the lake of fire includes "those who practice magic arts" (Revelation 21:8).

COUNSEL FROM GOD'S WORD

If you have dabbled with the occult in the past, or are presently addicted to its deceitful practices, you need to take this step-by-step process for deliverance.

1. Acknowledge that the occult is evil.

As Christians, we should love what God loves, and hate what He hates.

Our ultimate desire should be to please God, not others (1 Thessalonians 2:4) who may lead us astray. So, no matter what others have told you, you need to agree with God that the practices of the occult are evil and harmful, because they deny God's power and seek to tap into other, unseen forces.

2. Repent of and abandon any past involvement with the occult.

The Bible says, "unless you repent, you too will all perish" (Luke 13:3). Repentance includes abandoning past sin, and walking in a new direction. Proof that repentance has taken place involves not going back to one's former ways of sinning.

3. Reaffirm your faith in God as the only true God.

Occultic practices deny the sovereignty of the Lord, refusing to acknowledge that He is the one and only true God. The Lord Himself is clear: "I am the first and I am the last; apart from me there is no God" (Isaiah 44:6b).

In that same chapter, God reaffirms His exclusive right to be called God: "You are my witnesses. Is there any God besides me? No, there is no other Rock; I know not one" (Isaiah 44:8).

Again, a few verses later, He says: "I am the Lord, and there is no other; apart from me there is no God" (Isaiah 45:5).

4. Recognize that it's not important for us to know what's in the future, but to know Him who holds the future.

Whatever the future may bring, God has promised: "Never will I leave you; never will I forsake you" (Hebrews 13:5).

When Peter asked the Lord what the future held for the apostle John, Jesus replied: "what is that to you?" (John 21:22). God doesn't want us all concerned about the future. That's why Jesus said in the sermon on the mount:

> "So do not worry, saying, 'What shall we eat?' or 'What shall we drink?' or 'What shall we wear?' For the pagans run after all these things, and your heavenly Father knows that you need them" (Matthew 6:31-32).

5. Remember, nothing in the occult can add to what you have in Christ.

When you have Jesus Christ, you have everything. He told us plainly:

"The thief [the devil] comes only to steal and kill and destroy; I
have come that they may have life, and have it to the full" (John
10:10).

The apostle Paul adds: "you have been given fullness in Christ"
(Colossians 2:10), but warns:

See to it that no one takes you captive through hollow and deceptive philosophy, which depends on human tradition and the basic
principles on this world rather than on Christ (Colossians 2:8).

Nothing the occult offers can increase your quality or length of life. Jesus
alone offers true life! And forget consulting a medium or witch to find out the
deep secrets of life. God's Word contains all we need to know. It alone is reliable, powerful, and completely true.

6. Get into a Bible study, and immerse yourself in the Word of God.

We're commanded by God to hear His Word, read it, study it, memorize
it, meditate on it, and obey it. God's Word alone will keep you from falling into
error. Follow a systematic reading plan that gets you into God's Word every day
and through the Bible every year.

Studying God's Word isn't supposed to be a solo act. Paul writes: "Let the
word of Christ dwell in you richly as you teach and admonish one another"
(Colossians 3:16). Join a local church, and place yourself under the authority
and care of godly leaders who will hold you accountable.

Ted was very fortunate. We burned the occult materials he and Rich had
brought in. Ted not only repented of dabbling in this very dangerous and
demonic area, he also trusted Christ for salvation and was discipled by one of
the godly young men in the church. His testimony today is one of thanksgiving that he got out of the occult while he still could.

If you are dabbling in the occult, no matter how "innocent" your involvement may be, stop immediately, repent, and turn your life over to the Lord. He alone can "give you the desire of your heart" (Psalm 20:4).

■ ■ ■ ■ ■

More biblical counsel

1 TIMOTHY 4:1-5

JAMES 4:17

EPHESIANS 6:10-18

2 CORINTHIANS 10:3-5

ROMANS 8:38

MATTHEW 12:24-29

Seeking God's Will

Do not conform any longer to the pattern of this world,
but be transformed by the renewing of
your mind. Then you will be able to test and approve
what God's will is—his good, pleasing and perfect will.

ROMANS 12:2

■ ■ ■ ■ ■

Beverly blurted it out. "Pastor, I must know the will of God for my life! I can't go on anymore until I know it." We arranged a time for her and her husband to come in. She seemed distraught as she unfolded the conflicting plans she wanted to pursue.

In one breath, Beverly felt God calling her to cross-cultural missions, probably in Latin America. In the next breath, she felt a "tug" (as she put it) to open a house for troubled teenage girls. She then told me of a burden she had to counsel women, especially women married to non-Christian men. Her husband sat in silence as she went down the list.

After rambling for about thirty minutes, Beverly finally lifted up her hands in resignation and said, "Pastor, how can I know the will of God?"

Beverly's question is probably one of the most common I'm asked as a pastor. Knowing the will of God for one's life seems to be the paramount thing many sincere Christian people want. "If I can just know God's will for my life," one young man said to me, "I can handle just about anything that comes down the pike." I think that same feeling is shared by many people. Questions about the will of God often get quite specific. Most people want to know the will of God concerning:

- which school they should attend;
- which courses they should take;
- which vocation they should enter;
- which job they should pursue;
- which friends they should have;
- whom they should date and marry;
- where they should live.

Something in all of us wants a sign, a signal, some kind of definite indication from God showing which options we should pursue, what choices we should make.

Like Beverly, many become almost ill worrying so much about whether or not they are "in" the will of God.

COUNSEL FROM GOD'S WORD

The Bible has an answer for every challenge we face in life. Knowing God's will certainly is no exception. In fact, Scripture is the very best place to look!

GOD'S WILL REVEALED FOR ALL OF US

1. It is God's will that we be saved.

The Lord Jesus Christ told His disciples clearly:

"For my Father's will is that everyone who looks to the Son and believes in him shall have eternal life, and I will raise him up on the last day" (John 6:40).

The apostle Paul told Timothy that God "wants all men to be saved" (2 Timothy 2:4). Peter affirmed this same truth by saying the Lord "is patient with you, not wanting anyone to perish, but everyone to come to repentance" (2 Peter 3:9).

(If you aren't sure you are saved yet, settle the issue today! Turn to chapter 13, Doubting One's Salvation.)

2. It is God's will that we live holy lives.

Practical holiness is the will of God for all who have trusted Him for salvation. "It is God's will that you should be sanctified.... For God did not call us to be impure, but to live a holy life" (1 Thessalonians 4:3, 7).

3. It is God's will that we work diligently at our jobs.

As witnesses to a watching world, God wants us to be the best workers we can be:

> . . .obey your earthly masters with respect and fear, and with sincerity of heart, just as you would obey Christ. Obey them not only to win their favor when their eye is on you, but like slaves of Christ, doing the will of God from your heart (Ephesians 6:5-6).

4. It is God's will that we obey the governmental authorities.

As Christians, we have an obligation to be law-abiding citizens. The apostle Peter says:

> Submit yourselves for the Lord's sake to every authority instituted among men: whether to the king, as the supreme authority, or to governors, who are sent by him to punish those who do wrong and to commend those who do right. For it is God's will that by doing good you should silence the ignorant talk of foolish men (1 Peter 2:13-15).

5. It is God's will that we be Spirit-filled.

When we receive Jesus Christ, we are given the gift of the Holy Spirit (Acts 2:38). He became ours the moment we believed in Christ (Ephesians 1:13). In fact, if we don't have the Holy Spirit, we're not one of Christ's yet (Romans 8:9).

Even though all Christians are indwelt by the Holy Spirit, we're commanded to be completely Spirit-filled:

Therefore, do not be foolish, but understand what the Lord's will
is. Do not get drunk on wine, which leads to debauchery. Instead,
be filled with the Spirit (Ephesians 5:17-18).

To be "filled" with the Holy Spirit doesn't mean we get more of Him, but
that He finally gets all of us! It is a matter of control, allowing the Holy Spirit
who is resident in our life to be president, commander-in-chief.

All five points just listed speak of our personal relationships with God. It's
clear the Lord wants a personal relationship with each of us.

But what about those particular areas in life where Scripture doesn't say,
"Thus saith the Lord"? Thankfully, we can still turn to God's Word to get
answers to specific questions like:

- Should I buy a car?
- Which car should I buy?
- Should I get married?
- Whom should I marry?
- Should I buy a house?
- Which house should I buy?
- Should I get a new job?
- Which new job should I get?
- Should I have children?
- How many children should I have?
- Should I use birth control?

GOD'S REVEALED WILL FOR ME

1. Before you search the Scriptures, ask God for wisdom.

Echo the words of King David, who wanted to know God's will for his
life and prayed:

Show me your ways, O Lord, teach me your paths; guide me in
your truth and teach me, for you are God my Savior (Psalm 25:8).

Scripture repeatedly teaches that God will show us His will, if we ask
Him. The Lord told the prophet Jeremiah: "Call to me and I will answer you

and tell you great and unsearchable things you do not know" (Jeremiah 33:3).

God wants us to call on Him:

> If any of you lacks wisdom, he should ask God, who gives gener-
> ously to all without finding fault, and it will be given to him. But
> when he asks he must believe and not doubt, because he who
> doubts is like a wave of the sea, blown and tossed by the wind
> (James 1:5-6).

2. Make a decision to obey God's will before you learn what it is.

Many people want to know God's will for their lives before they make a decision whether or not they will obey it. But Jesus told His disciples:

> "If anyone chooses to do God's will, he will find out whether my
> teaching comes from God or whether I speak on my own" (John
> 7:17).

3. Trust the sovereignty of God.

God promises to direct your steps aright. Trust Him! He promises: "I will instruct you and teach you in the way you should go; I will counsel you and watch over you" (Psalm 32:8).

Solomon wisely urges us:

> Trust in the Lord with all your heart and lean not on your own
> understanding; in all your ways acknowledge him, and he will
> make your paths straight (Proverbs 3:5-6).

4. Pay close attention to closed doors.

God sometimes reveals His particular will to us by closing doors. Before you make a decision, ask God to close the door to any option outside His will.

In Numbers 22:21-31 we read about one of the most dramatic roadblocks in history. God was angry with the prophet Balaam, and sent an angel to block his way. When his donkey stopped in her tracks, all Balaam knew to do was beat her. When the angel blocked his way two more times, Balaam beat his donkey again, even though the beast was only obeying the Lord. Then God finally opened Balaam's eyes to see what the donkey saw! Sadly, he still persisted in going his own way, and a few chapters later met with destruction (Numbers 31:8).

Another example of God closing doors is recorded by Luke:

> Paul and his companions traveled throughout the region of
> Phrygia and Galatia, having been kept by the Holy Spirit from
> preaching the word in the province of Asia. When they came to
> the border of Mysia, they tried to enter Bithynia, but the Spirit of
> Jesus would not allow them to (Acts 16:6-7).

We don't know why, but God didn't want Paul and his team preaching the gospel in the province of Asia, so He blocked the way. Paul probably never was told why. If God closes a door, trust Him and keep moving ahead until He opens just the right door.

5. Recognize that God chooses sometimes not to reveal His ways to us.

If we don't have a clear word from God about a particular situation, we simply need to follow what Scripture does say. Moses wrote:

> The secret things belong to the Lord our God, but the things
> revealed belong to us and our children forever, that we may fol-
> low all the words of this law (Deuteronomy 29:29).

6. As long as we are walking in God's revealed will, filled with His Holy Spirit, we should proceed with the desires of our hearts.

One young woman told me she believed God was calling her to the mission field, but she didn't know where. I asked her, "Where would you like to go?"

She replied, "I would like to go to India. I even dream about it. It's the one place I would especially like to go." So I told her, "Then go to India, and get on with it!" It's perfectly fine to pursue such desires, so long as they don't conflict with any biblical principles.

The psalmist urges us: "Delight yourself in the Lord and he will give you the desires of your heart" (Psalm 37:4). The secret is delighting ourselves in the Lord alone. When we do, He has no problem giving us the desires of our heart.

7. Value the wise counsel of others.

We need to seek the godly counsel of people committed to following God's will in their own lives. Never trust your inward convictions, if godly people who know you well advise you to go a different direction.

Solomon pressed this truth home when he wrote: "Plans fail for lack of counsel, but with many advisers they succeed" (Proverbs 15:22). And, "For lack of guidance a nation falls, but many advisers make victory sure" (Proverbs 11:14).

We all need the straightforward, prayerful counsel of friends who love us and are seeking first the kingdom of God in their own lives.

8. Evaluate your answers to the tough questions.

Before pursuing a course of action, we need to place that decision under the searchlight of several important questions:

- Will this be beneficial for me, my health, and my family?
- Will this keep me free from any taint of compromise?
- Will this glorify God and bring honor to Him?
- Will this be a wise financial decision?
- Will this enhance my career and other stated goals?
- Will this help me be a good steward of what God has given me?
- Will this enhance my marriage (if married)?

If you can answer "yes" to all these questions, fine. If not, reconsider your intended course of action.

What about Beverly?

After receiving prayerful counsel, she decided to bloom where she's planted. As a wife, mother, and church member, she decided to make her ministry count in those three arenas. I doubt if she'll ever go to Latin America as a missionary, or open a house for troubled teenage girls, but she has perfect peace about what God wants her to do.

God's revealed will is in Scripture. God's daily will can be found by prayer and wise counsel. God's hidden will won't be divulged, but we can trust Him for the future.

■ ■ ■ ■ ■

More biblical counsel

PSALM 40:8

PSALM 119:105

GENESIS 24:27

PHILIPPIANS 4:6-9

JOHN 16:13

ISAIAH 32:17

I SAMUEL 15:22

JOHN 14:15

JOHN 14:23

JAMES 1:22

PSALM 37:3-5

PSALM 84:11

PSALM 86:11

ISAIAH 14:24

ISAIAH 26:3

ISAIAH 32:8

ISAIAH 41:10

Suicide

Submit yourselves, then, to God.
Resist the devil, and he will flee from you.

JAMES 4:7

■ ■ ■ ■ ■

When the phone rang, I sat up and glanced at the clock. It was 2:30 in the morning. The lady at the other end of the phone was a nurse in the psychiatric unit of a local hospital. She sounded urgent, saying I had better come immediately.

When I arrived at the psych unit, I was taken to a dimly lit private room. In bed with both wrists bandaged tightly was a late teen I'll call Debbie. She moved in and out of consciousness, and in the hallway the nurse told me her chances looked bleak.

Among teenagers, suicide has become America's second leading cause of death. Many coroners will not rule a death a suicide if the deceased didn't leave a note. Still, every day an average of at least eighteen teenagers take their own lives. Reliable sources estimate more than one thousand teens make a serious attempt at killing themselves each day.

Furthermore, it is estimated that the frequency of teenage suicide has increased more than 400 percent since the early 1950s. The number of non-teen suicides is also dramatically on the rise.

WHY DO PEOPLE ATTEMPT SUICIDE?

1. Some attempt to take their life because they are in a pit of depression and gloom, and see life getting only worse, not better.

They see suicide as the only way to escape the horrible depressive feelings in which they've become mired. They have taken their eyes off the Lord and lost all hope.

2. Overwhelming guilt causes some people to try to end their lives.

In some cases people would rather face death than risk being "discovered." Perhaps they've been involved in an affair, or embezzled money at work, or become addicted to drugs. Rather than have their family and friends discover the truth, they decide to end it all.

3. Financial loss causes some to take their lives.

Scores of businessmen jumped to their deaths during the 1929 stock market crash. They chose death rather than face poverty and debt the rest of their lives. Sometimes people who lose an expensive home by flood, fire, or the folly of co-signing someone else's loan decide death is to be preferred over suffering through such a loss. Some women who have gone through a divorce, and lost all sense of financial security, in desperation also turn to suicide.

4. Some commit suicide because of health problems.

The issue of medically assisted suicides is a topic of hot debate in our country today. People who have incurable cancer, who are severely injured in auto accidents, or who are paraplegic sometimes choose to take their lives. They cannot bear the thought of living out the rest of their lives in a wheelchair.

5. Loss of a loved one causes some to contemplate suicide.

Some feel they cannot handle the overwhelming grief they feel, and decide they cannot go on living without their loved one.

6. People take their lives because of low Christ-esteem.

They fail to realize they have any sense of worth in Christ. Notice I didn't say *self*-esteem. We need to base our esteem on the worth and dignity we have in Jesus Christ alone.

The one common denominator in all suicide attempts is the person's utter loss of all hope. It is the overwhelming sense that the situation is beyond repair and will only grow worse. A suicidal person is given over to total despair. He not only sees no way out of his predicament, but sometimes doesn't even want to see a way out.

FALSE NOTIONS ABOUT SUICIDE

1. "There are usually no warnings before someone attempts suicide."

Many believe suicides happen suddenly, with little or no warning. Nothing could be farther from the truth. A suicide attempt is often the culmination of struggles that have been brewing for months, even years. The person contemplating suicide leaves clues all along the way; we must be perceptive enough to pick up on them.

2. "People who leave hints about contemplating suicide usually don't attempt it."

Not so. We're told that four out of five people who attempt suicide have made previous attempts. Some wrongly believe if you show a suicidal person any interest or pity, you're only feeding that person's ego and pride. When people threaten to take their lives, it's a cry for someone to respond.

3. "Suicide is somehow genetic, and runs in the family."

Again, this is a common myth that simply isn't true. There is no evidence to support such a claim. Sometimes, however, families are so devastated when one member takes his or her life that someone else in the family later attempts suicide. This isn't because "suicide runs in the genes," but because suicide is so devastating to other family members.

4. "People who threaten suicide cannot be talked out of it."

Wrong again! Studies show the more earnestly someone offers a suicidal person hope, the higher the probability the suicidal person won't take his or her life. In most cases when someone is contemplating suicide, the scales have tipped toward how hopeless the situation is. If someone just talks to them, and shows them reasons why there still is a reason for living, they often can tip the scales and save that person's life.

5. "If someone commits suicide, he or she is either mentally ill or not a Christian."

This myth prevents a lot of people from receiving help. The truth is, many sane and Christian people reach a place of despair and can see no way to go on. It can happen to anyone, Christian or non-Christian. Elijah was one of the greatest prophets of all time, yet even he almost threw in the towel at one point (1 Kings 19:4).

6. "Most people who take their lives are very sick or elderly and have only a short time to live anyway."

Sorry, but statistics indicate that by far the majority of suicides occur among people between the ages of fifteen and twenty-four.

7. "People who threaten to kill themselves are only seeking attention and don't really mean it."

Again, this is a blatant myth. Most people who talk about taking their life carry out their threat. That is precisely why we should never ignore a hint, let alone a threat that someone may attempt suicide.

IMPORTANT!

If you're contemplating taking your own life, please, immediately divulge your plans to a trusted friend, pastor, or professional Christian counselor. Don't keep such thoughts bottled up inside you. Ask for prayer and counsel. Then, together, consider the following truths from God's Word, the Bible.

COUNSEL FROM GOD'S WORD

1. Your life is a gift from God!

The Bible says about each life: "Sons are a heritage from the Lord, children a reward from him" (Psalm 127:3). The Hebrew word "heritage" means gift or trust. You, yourself, exist by God's design. You weren't an accident. Your life is a gift from an all-wise, all-powerful God. To destroy that gift is an affront to the One who made you and loves you.

2. To destroy yourself is to commit murder.

It's a direct violation of the sixth commandment, "You shall not murder" (Exodus 20:13). There is a finality to murder. There are no reruns or second takes. Also, once you have murdered yourself, there is no opportunity to repent before God for what you've done, let alone apologize to your family and friends.

3. If your attempt doesn't work, you have more than likely maimed your body for life.

The Bible teaches us that our body is a temple of the Holy Spirit and deserves special honor:

> Do you not know that your body is a temple of the Holy Spirit,
> who is in you, whom you have received from God? You are not
> your own; you were bought at a price. Therefore honor God with
> your body (1 Corinthians 6:19-20).

Whether your attempt works or doesn't, you will violate this direct command from God's Word.

4. Suicide may appear to be an out for you, but you'll bring agony on your family for the rest of their lives.

I realize that in a confused state of mind, one doesn't usually think of such things. But suicide is the ultimate in selfish acts, because it confirms that you're only thinking of yourself. "For none of us lives to himself alone and none of us dies to himself alone' (Romans 14:7).

The grief, the agony, the unanswered questions you will leave behind are a terrible price to pay for something you think will put you out of your misery.

5. There is a better alternative to suicide.

It's called trusting in God to work out the complex strands in your life. We see a wonderful example of this in the Old Testament.

When David and his men returned to the city where they were living, they found it destroyed by fire, and their wives and sons and daughters taken captive by the enemy. David's men were so distraught some even talked of stoning him. It was probably one of the very lowest times in David's entire life.

David's solution when he came to the end of his rope? Suicide? No, though I'm sure it crossed his mind. In all probability, he was tempted by Satan to kill himself, perhaps as a futile attempt to "save face." Instead, "David found strength in the Lord his God" (1 Samuel 30:6b).

The end of the story is one of rejoicing after a great victory. David and his men rescued their families and recaptured one hundred percent of all that had been stolen. Why all this good fortune? David trusted God rather than take his own life.

The Lord has promised to respond when you go to Him with problems bigger than you. You won't be let down, disappointed, or turned away (Jeremiah 33:3).

6. Remember, whatever you're going through is not permanent!

Whatever trial, hardship, disappointment, or situation you may be going through will not last forever. That's why David could write: "weeping may remain for a night, but rejoicing comes in the morning" (Psalm 30:5b).

God has a way of redeeming our circumstances, and restoring our losses. He could promise the nation of Israel: "I will repay you for the years the locusts have eaten" (Joel 2:25a). The Lord has a way of bringing back the money, honor, character, marriage, health, profits, joy, peace, and tranquility you may have lost.

Physically, your situation may never change. Perhaps you're disabled or disfigured after surgery to remove a cancerous lump. But what about your heart attitude? If you're going through the depths of depression, don't forget that God is *Jehovah-Rapha*, the Everlasting One who heals you (Exodus 15:26).

7. Thievery is involved in suicide.

When you take your own life, you are stealing. You are robbing the world of all the potential wrapped up in you.

A few years back, a popular children's song said, "I am a great big bundle of possibilities." That's exactly what you are, and to take your own life is to eliminate those potentials from ever becoming realities.

If you are a teenager, your hands may someday be the hands of a surgeon or concert pianist; your tongue may be that of a famous orator, instructor or preacher; your eyes may look through electron microscopes to hasten an end to cancer; your mind may be that of a famous research scientist, cyberspace guru, or theologian. To take your life cancels all those possibilities.

The Bible says we are "fearfully and wonderfully made" (Psalm 139:14). Every individual is endowed with his own set of giftedness and potential. Premature death by suicide assures we will never become what God intended us to be.

8. If you attempt suicide, you usurp God and put yourself in His place.

To take your life in your own hands is to assume you're greater than God. That's absurd, of course. The Bible makes it clear that the day of our death is known to God, and nothing will change that.

David praised God that, "All the days ordained for me were written in your book before one of them came to be" (Psalm 139:16). Job declared:

> Man's days are determined; you have decreed the number of his months, and have set limits he cannot exceed (Job 14:5).

For us, then, to take our own lives before our "allotted number of months come to an end" (Job 21:21) is tantamount to saying we know more than God about our own personal welfare.

You may be wondering about Debbie. She recommitted her life to the Lord, joined a Bible study group at our church, and got a good job. She's in her mid-twenties now, is surrounded by friends who care about her, and is thankful to the Lord for all the reasons He's given her to live.

■ ■ ■ ■ ■

More biblical counsel

HEBREWS 13:5B

MATTHEW 11:28-30

1 PETER 5:7-11
2 CORINTHIANS 4:7-18
PSALM 23
PSALM 55:22
PSALM 56:3-4
PSALM 27:1
PSALM 31
PSALM 62:1-2
ISAIAH 40:28-31
ISAIAH 41:10
ISAIAH 43:1-3
PSALM 37:4-5
PSALM 37:25
PSALM 42:5-11
PSALM 46:1-3
PSALM 73:25-26

Terminal Illness

But he said to me,
"My grace is sufficient for you,
for my power is made perfect in weakness."
Therefore I will boast all the
more gladly about my weaknesses, so
that Christ's power may rest on me.

2 CORINTHIANS 12:9

·····

ary was my associate pastor. He was twenty-nine years old, and newly married. Full of enthusiasm, humor, life, and joy, he was marvelous with our teens. Shortly after coming on staff, I noticed Gary began to walk more slowly. He stilled laughed at everything, but I could read something else through his laughter.

One day Gary called in sick, telling me he had no energy. The next day he seemed better and was back to work. A few days later, he lost his energy again, and this continued off and on for the next two months.

Finally Gary confided in me that he had terrible pain in his stomach, and went to see a doctor. This particular doctor examined him and told him it was all in his head. But the pain continued and worsened.

Finally I took Gary to a larger city and had a specialist examine him. He felt the need for exploratory surgery. He was in surgery some eight hours. When the doctor met his wife and me in the waiting room, we both knew by the look on his face the news wasn't good.

"I'm sorry," he told Jean, "but your husband has a very large tumor that takes up most of his stomach and lower bowel track, and it's inoperable. It's growing very rapidly and neither chemotherapy nor radiation can stop it at this point." She began to weep. To complicate matters, Gary and Jean were in the midst of final proceedings for adopting their first child.

I walked with Gary through his "death sentence," and from it learned some invaluable lessons.

THE GAMUT OF EMOTIONS

I've learned through the years—not only with Gary, but with many others—that individuals facing a terminal illness seem to go through a sequential gamut of emotions.

1. Euphoric optimism

This emotion follows the initial shock and disappointment, which is short-lived. I call it "euphoric" optimism because it seems to be just that. The victim seems ridiculously optimistic.

I remember Gary's remarks: "I'll beat this thing." "God will heal me." "The doctors have been wrong before, and they're wrong again about this."

As his confidant, best friend, pastor, and colleague, I thought to myself: "I've got to straighten Gary's thinking out. He's not facing reality. He's in a world of illusion."

But on second thought I saw I was walking into an area where I had no business treading. I realized to prick his bubble would be to destroy any hope he might have, so I "believed" along with him, hoping, of course that he was right.

2. Anger

I'll never forget the day I visited Gary in the hospital only to hear him say: "Who am I fooling? I'm not going to get well. I'm going to die! What kind of God have I been serving that would let one of His servants die so young?"

As I let Gary talk, I could see the fire in his eyes. He went on to complain about the fact that he would never live to see his daughter grow up. His pain only accentuated his raging anger.

3. Acceptance

After a while, Gary's anger was gone. In its place was a stark acceptance that he wouldn't live much longer. This is a time to get things in order. It's a time to spend with those you love the most. True, sometimes even morphine won't kill the pain. In his agony, Gary still asked the tough questions, but he clung to his faith in God's sovereignty.

I remember the day Gary said to me, "It's finally hitting me. I've got cancer. It's not going away. I'm going to die." Every time he looked at his gaunt face in the mirror, that statement was confirmed.

These stages and the whole gamut of changing emotions come at different times for different people. Some stages last longer than others, and the feelings often overlap.

COUNSEL FROM GOD'S WORD

If you or a loved one are facing what could be a terminal illness, it's good to know God has not left us to flounder. There are steps to take and truths to believe that will get us through the hard times.

1. First, realize that everyone is "terminal."

One man went to his doctor recently and discovered he has cancer. "The doctor sat me down and told me that I was terminal," he told me. "I replied, 'So are you, Doc.'"

Scripture says, "man is destined to die once" (Hebrews 9:27). It's an unavoidable consequence of the fall of man (Romans 5:12). Death is certain because sin is the ultimate terminal illness (Romans 6:23).

As fallen mortal beings, God never intended that we live on this earth within our current body forever. That would be the worse fate possible, if you think about it! As Christians, we have the glorious promise that someday we'll get a new body, perfectly suited for eternity (2 Corinthians 5:1). What a precious promise from God's Word!

2. Remember God alone has appointed the day of our death.

The Bible is very clear on this. It's even told us what to expect as far as life expectancy is concerned:

The length of our days is seventy years—
or eighty, if we have strength; yet their
span is but trouble and sorrow, for they
quickly pass, and we fly away (Psalm 90:10).

No wonder a couple verses later, Moses asks God to help us "number our days aright, that we may gain a heart of wisdom" (Psalm 90:12).

God sovereignly controls the length of our stay on this earth. Job affirmed: "Man's days are determined; you have decreed the number of his months and have set limits he cannot exceed" (Job 14:5).

God knows exactly how long each of us will live. Job observed there is a time when a man's "allotted months come to an end" (Job 21:21). Solomon said there is "a time to be born and a time to die" (Ecclesiastes 3:2).

When our "allotted" time is up, whether at age thirty or age eighty, God will sovereignly take us home to be with Him. Unless Jesus Christ comes back in our lifetime, we all have a rendezvous with death. It's one appointment we will not miss.

Only on rare occasions has God elected to extend a man's life beyond his original limit. Several were raised from the dead in the days of Elijah and Elisha, and several more during Jesus Christ's earthly ministry. In addition, when King Hezekiah was told by the prophet Isaiah that he was going to die, Hezekiah cried out to God, who replied:

"This is what the Lord, the God of your
father David, says: I have heard your
prayer and seen your tears; I will heal
you. On the third day from now you will
go up to the temple of the Lord. I will
add fifteen years to your life…"
(2 Kings 20:5-6).

But even on this occasion, God knew ahead of time exactly what He was going to do. Our days are truly numbered by the Lord, our Creator and Sustainer. Our appointed time is truly in His hand!

Solomon mused on the mystery of life, but hit the nail on the head when he said: "Like the fool, the wise man too must die" (Ecclesiastes 2:16b).

3. Understand that disease and pain give God's grace room to work in us.

When Paul prayed three times for his "thorn" to be removed, God sovereignly chose not to remove it. Though no one really knows what Paul's thorn was, most believe it was a physical disease, perhaps glaucoma or a form of hepatitis.

Don't get me wrong. God didn't forsake Paul. Just the opposite!

He said to me, "My grace is sufficient for you,
for my power is made perfect in weakness."
Therefore I will boast all the more gladly
about my weaknesses, so that Christ's power
may rest on me" (2 Corinthians 12:9).

In other words, Paul was content to live with his illness, since it drove him to a deeper reliance on the Lord—far deeper than he would have had without the illness.

Similarly, if having a terminal illness that enables me to more fully experience the grace of God—in a way I probably never would have otherwise experienced—I truly have reason to thank God for my illness.

I'm not sure why God wants us to give thanks even for terminal illnesses, but He does. Scripture teaches our thanksgiving isn't to be dependent on our circumstances. Instead, we are to "give thanks in all circumstances, for this is God's will for you in Christ Jesus" (1 Thessalonians 5:18).

4. Realize God has a sovereign plan for our futures, no matter what happens.

No matter what our health may be like, we can live out our remaining days enjoying God's sovereign care. Even if we don't understand the "way" He has chosen for us, we can walk through each and every day with thanksgiving in our hearts.

In the midst of incredible pain and despair, Job acknowledged both God's sovereignty and goodness:

But he knows the way that I take;
when he has tested me, I will come
forth as gold (Job 23:10).

Which of us can ignore what is perhaps the most precious promise of the whole Bible?

"For I know the plans I have for you," declares
the Lord, "plans to prosper you and not to harm
you, plans to give you hope and a future"
(Jeremiah 29:11).

God's sovereignty is never in question, whether we face a terminal illness or not. Scripture promises: "If we endure, we will also reign with him" (2 Timothy 2:12).

Whatever suffering you may be going through right now is no accident. God makes no mistakes. Romans 5:3-5 tell us that suffering produces character, which in turn produces hope that never disappoints. In that alone, we can take great confidence.

5. God wants you to use your terminal illness to help others.

Our world would be poorer if people like Amy Carmichael, Fanny Crosby, George Matheson, and others had not seen their suffering as a tool God placed in their hands to touch other people's lives.

God has given you a terminal illness for a similar reason.

Someone well acquainted with grief once wrote:

Out of the presses of pain
Cometh the soul's best wine;
And the eyes that have shed no rain
Can shed but little shine.

The apostle Paul said it this way:

Now I want you to know, brothers, that what has
happened to me has really served to advance the
gospel. As a result, it has become clear throughout
the whole palace guard and to everyone else that
I am in chains for Christ. Because of my chains,
most of the brothers in the Lord have been
encouraged to speak the word of God more
courageously and fearlessly (Philippians 1:12-14).

Paul could say, in effect: "I'm suffering, but God is using it to bless others!" By God's grace, may you be able to say that, too.

6. Understand suffering does a great deal of good in our lives.

a. God uses suffering to refine, perfect, strengthen, and keep us from
falling (Psalm 66:8-9, Hebrews 2:10, Hebrews 12:10).

b. Suffering teaches us humility (2 Corinthians 12:7).

c. Suffering brings believers together in unity (Revelation 1:9).

d. Suffering produces a broken and contrite heart, which is well pleasing
to God (Psalm 51:16-17).

e. Suffering qualifies us to help others who suffer (2 Corinthians 1:3-11).

f. Suffering forces us to rely on God (Psalm 11:1, Psalm 14:6).

g. Suffering increases our faith (Genesis 22, Psalm 46:10).

h. Suffering breaks the will of the rebellious (Revelation 11:13).

i. Suffering stretches our hope (Job 13:14-15).

j. Suffering leads us to repentance (Psalm 32, 2 Corinthians 7:5-11).

What about my associate, Gary?

He died, close to the time frame the doctors said he would. I will never
forget his last words to me: "Bob, they say I have a terminal illness. The illness
is terminal, I'm not. Jesus said I would live forever with Him."

That was Gary's hope clear to the end. That can be yours, too. Perhaps
the greatest affirmation those suffering from a terminal illness can make is to
say: "For to me, to live is Christ and to die is gain" (Philippians 1:21).

■ ■ ■ ■ ■

More biblical counsel

EXODUS 3:7

JOB 30:16

PSALM 119:50

PSALM 46:1

PSALM 37:5-6

PSALM 37:25

PSALM 23

PSALM 56:3-4

PSALM 56:8

PSALM 73

ISAIAH 43:1-3

JOHN 14:1-6

REVELATION 22:1-5

1 CORINTHIANS 15

1 PETER 5:7

HEBREWS 13:14

2 CORINTHIANS 4:7-18

2 CORINTHIANS 5:1-6

The Unpardonable Sin

But whoever blasphemes against the
Holy Spirit will never be forgiven;
he is guilty of an eternal sin.

MARK 3:29

■■■■■

Syrian by birth, from age four Tal had grown up in America. I first met him when he and his fiancée made an appointment with me to discuss their upcoming wedding. Tal was twenty-eight years old, very quiet, an electrical engineer graduate who held a responsible job with a large and successful firm in our city.

During our first ten minutes together, as I asked Tal and his fiancée about their spiritual background, he hedged a lot. It was soon apparent he didn't want to talk about his spiritual life at all. We went on to other things, but before agreeing to marry them, I made an appointment for lunch with Tal. It was then, with head hung low, that he told me, "I'm sure I've committed the unpardonable sin, and thus God wouldn't want to have me now." I asked for details.

It turned out that in his early twenties, Tal was invited to church by a friend. He liked the services, and even went forward to receive Jesus

257

Christ. For a period of a few months, he grew, went weekly to a disciple-ship class, and thoroughly enjoyed his newfound faith.

During this time Tal met a girl at that church, and they began dating. One evening, Tal made the mistake of going to her apartment, staying all night. In his words, "I knew what I was doing was wrong, yet I felt I couldn't stop myself. I lost my virginity that night, and cannot shake the guilt. I believe I also blasphemed the Holy Spirit, which is the unforgivable sin."

What actually happened to Tal? From his perspective, it was all over. In his mind, he had lost his salvation, committing a sin so horrible he could never be forgiven. We talked till three in the afternoon! Did Tal commit the unpardonable sin, or not?

I've discovered that many, like Tal, are confused regarding exactly what the unpardonable sin is all about. The confusion ranges from people who constantly feel they've committed that sin, to people who don't believe in the unpardonable sin.

IS THERE AN UNPARDONABLE SIN?

Some Bible scholars who love the Lord believe there is no such thing as an unpardonable sin. They maintain that to say God won't forgive a certain sin is to go against the very nature of God, "who forgives all your sins" (Psalm 103:3).

These same men teach that to say there is an unpardonable sin is to deny the free, abundant grace God wants to lavish on us. They say that for God to withhold His forgiveness from us, no matter what the sin, is a denial that God says, "I have loved you with an everlasting love" (Jeremiah 31:3).

They also argue that to acknowledge a sin God won't forgive is to suggest there is something that God cannot do, further running contrary to the nature of God. After all, God is both all-powerful and all-loving.

From my own study, however, I believe Scripture clearly teaches there is an unpardonable sin. The question isn't "Does this doctrine sound right?" but "Is it what God Himself has declared?"

Generally speaking, Scripture teaches that before God's grace—His free, unmerited favor—can be appropriated, we must meet the condition He has established for receiving it. The condition is simple: It's agreeing with God that there is nothing within us that somehow partially merits His grace.

We qualify for God's grace by admitting we don't deserve it. We qualify by acknowledging that as sinners, we have no claim on God's forgiveness and love. We qualify by thanking God that, despite our sin, He is still willing to offer His grace to us.

The unpardonable sin is a sin that prevents us from qualifying for the grace of God. And, since we can only be saved by grace, the deliberate refusal to accept that free, unmerited gift automatically blocks God's forgiveness from us. As I explain below, that and that alone is the unpardonable sin.

COUNSEL FROM GOD'S WORD

If you feel you may have committed the unpardonable sin, the first thing you need to do is check Scripture and find out what Jesus Himself said this sin actually is.

WHAT JESUS TAUGHT

In Matthew's Gospel, Jesus says:

"And so I tell you, every sin and blasphemy will be
forgiven men, but the blasphemy against the Spirit
will not be forgiven. Anyone who speaks against the
Son of Man will be forgiven, but anyone who speaks
against the Holy Spirit will not be forgiven, either
in this age or the age to come"
(Matthew 12:31-32).

In Mark's account, Jesus says virtualy the same thing, with a slightly different emphasis:

"I tell you the truth, all the sins and blasphemies
of men will be forgiven them. But whoever blasphemes
against the Holy Spirit will never be forgiven. Anyone
who speaks a word against the Holy Spirit will not be
forgiven; he is guilty of an eternal sin"
(Mark 3:28-29).

The same statement is recorded in Luke 12:10. In these three accounts, what is Jesus saying?

1. All sins will be forgiven except one.

2. "Blasphemy" here is equated with speaking against the Holy Spirit.

3. Such blasphemy an "eternal" sin that has no forgiveness in this age or the age to come. It's obvious that Jesus is talking about a very serious sin, indeed.

Based on what Jesus taught, let's clarify, then, what the unpardonable sin is and is not.

WHAT THE UNPARDONABLE SIN IS NOT

1. It is not the "sin that leads to death."

The sin mentioned in 1 John 5:16 is one committed by a Christian that leads to physical death. The "sin that leads to death" mentioned in that passage is a pardonable sin, even though the person dies prematurely.

A good example of this is a drunk who repents, comes to Christ, and is forgiven. If his past sin destroyed his liver, he's forgiven, he's saved, but he's still going to an early grave.

Another example of this sin is a believer who blatantly sins against the Lord and is judged. We see examples of this in Numbers 16:1-35, Acts 5:1-11, and 1 Corinthians 11:30.

2. It is not sexual sin.

This sin is serious, whether it's committed by Christians or non-Christians. For the believer, it is certainly forgivable upon repentance. The Corinthian church was full of converted adulterers, fornicators, homosexuals who once had lived in immorality, but now were "washed and sanctified" (1 Corinthians 6:11).

3. It is not suicide or murder.

The taking of life, yours or someone else's, is most serious. But don't forget the apostle Paul himself had been a murderer (Acts 8:3, 9:1, 22:4, and 26:10). If a person is saved and takes his own life, it would have to be in a time of severe depression. But if he's truly saved, he'll go to heaven. If he's not a Christian and takes his own life, killing himself won't keep him out of heaven—his failure to accept Christ in this life will.

4. It is not grieving or quenching the Holy Spirit.

In 1 Thessalonians 5:19, Paul exhorts us not to quench the Spirit. In other words, we're to not "smother" or "put out the fire" of the Spirit. In Ephesians 4:30, he further exhorts us to not "grieve" the Spirit. Though Christians do both on occasion, they are forgiven because they are under the blood of Jesus, which cleanses them from all sin (1 John 1:7).

5. It is not blaspheming or denying Jesus.

Paul was a blasphemer in his pre-Christian days (1 Timothy 1:13), yet he was gloriously forgiven and saved. Jesus Himself said in Matthew 12:32 that anyone who speaks a word against the Son of Man will be forgiven.

6. Simply put, the unpardonable sin cannot be committed by a believer.

In God's Word, we're promised forgiveness for all the sins we commit as a believer (Acts 10:43, 1 John 1:7). We're also told that once we're saved, "no one can snatch us" out of God's hand (John 10:27-28). No sin we can commit as a believer can strip our salvation from us.

WHAT THE UNPARDONABLE SIN IS

Taking the above passages from Matthew, Mark, and Luke that describe the unpardonable sin in their context will help us understand exactly what Jesus taught about the "blasphemy against the Holy Spirit."

In these accounts, a man was brought to Jesus who was demon-possessed (Matthew 12:22). He was blind and mute. Jesus healed him and restored him to wholeness. Everyone marveled at this—except the hardened Pharisees, a very strict Jewish party. In anger, they charged Jesus with casting out the demons by the power and authority of Beelzebub, the prince of demons. In other words, they said he was doing his mighty works by the power of Satan, rather than God.

These "religious" leaders had reached such a low state of spiritual degeneracy that they called evil good, and good evil. They came to the bottom of a frightening spiritual downward spiral by repeatedly refusing to accept Jesus Christ as the promised Messiah. Their sin, then? Repeated rejection of Christ, until they were no longer able to accept Him for who He was.

The Bible clearly teaches in both the Old and New Testaments that it's the Holy Spirit who brings the truth of God to men. To every Jew, the Holy Spirit had two functions. First, He was the God-ordained vehicle by which God's final truth was brought to people. He was God's instrument in revelation. Second, the Holy Spirit alone enabled people to recognize truth when they saw it.

Thus, the Pharisees rejected God's only vehicle (means) of truth, thus cutting them off from hearing and seeing—and recognizing Jesus for who He was.

Today, the Holy Spirit still teaches believers all things (John 14:25). He not only makes known God's truth, but convicts us of our sin, so that we will accept God's truth and remedy (John 16:7). If we reject the Holy Spirit, both of these ministries are closed to us. We have cut off any means of God's truth flowing into us.

If I'm driving down the road, and a flagger attempts to wave me down to let me know the bridge ahead is flooded out, but I ignore him, I will plunge to my death. Why? Because I rejected the highway department's only means of communicating the truth of the situation to me.

To continually reject the messenger—the Holy Spirit—is to continually reject the message—gospel—which is able to save us. To reject the message is to reject repentance, and no repentance means no salvation. If we reject God's gift of salvation enough times, we reach a state where we are beyond being touched by the truth of the gospel. We've sealed our own destiny at this point.

So, yes, it is possible to commit the unpardonable sin today. The Lord has said, "My Spirit will not contend with man forever" (Genesis 6:3). There is a line beyond which God stops pleading with us once, through repeated rejections, we have hardened ourselves and thus become incapable of repenting.

The Bible says, "Seek the Lord while he may be found, call on Him while he is near" (Isaiah 55:5). The use of the word "while" suggests the window of salvation will not always remain open. It definitely closes for good if our repeated rejections prohibits God's truth from coming to us.

Conversely, what is the chief condition of receiving God's pardon? David explained: it is "a broken and contrite heart" (Psalm 51:17). The Lord Himself says:

"This is the one I esteem: he who is humble
and contrite in spirit, and trembles at my
word" (Isaiah 66:2b).

If a broken, repentant, and contrite heart is necessary for salvation, but we cut off the very means by which our hearts becomes broken and contrite, we then cut off any hope of being forgiven and thus saved.

So here is the downward spiral we all must avoid: If we reject God's only means by which we are made broken and contrite (the Holy Spirit), we remove ourselves from meeting the condition of pardon, which is sorrow for sin; without sorrow for sin, we cannot repent; unless we repent, we cannot be saved (Luke 13:3).

Who then commits the unpardonable sin? The person who repeatedly says "no" to Christ so many times that he becomes incapable of saying "yes."

What about Tal?

Had Tal committed the "unpardonable sin?" Emphatically not. The fact that he was troubled by his one case of sexual immorality proved he felt guilty before God, which proved the Holy Spirit was convicting him, which proved the Holy Spirit was getting through to him!

After about two hours in God's Word, Tal recommitted his life to

Christ, and began to live in victory, now that he knew he wasn't a "doomed" man.

IS IT TOO LATE?

Maybe you're saying, "But what about me? I'll be honest, I'm not a Christian yet. In fact, all these years I've rejected Christ. I now know I was wrong—is it too late for me to accept Him?"

No, it's not too late! Why? Because you have just admitted that you feel guilty. For that to be possible, you have not cut off God's only means of revealing truth to you through the Holy Spirit. And that means you have not blasphemed Him yet.

Give your heart to Jesus Christ right now! Before you put this book down, pray this prayer:

> *Dear Lord, I know I'm a sinner. I'm truly sorry for*
> *my sin, and believe Jesus died on the cross to save*
> *me. Lord Jesus, come into my heart. I accept You*
> *right now as my Lord and Savior. Amen.*

■ ■ ■ ■ ■

More biblical counsel

ROMANS 3:23

ROMANS 6:23

ISAIAH 59:2

PSALM 49:7

1 CORINTHIANS 15:3

ACTS 2:38

ACTS 3:19

ACTS 16:31

ROMANS 8:9-10

ROMANS 10:9-10

ROMANS 10:13

1 Corinthians 1:8-9

Philippians 1:6

1 John 1:9

Ephesians 1:7

1 Peter 1:18

1 John 5:12-13

Worry and
Anxiety

Do not be anxious about anything,
but in everything, by prayer and
petition, with thanksgiving,
present your requests to God.

PHILIPPIANS 4:6

■ ■ ■ ■ ■

I had no idea why I was having lunch with Ian. I only know his voice sounded desperate yet matter-of-fact when he called to make the appointment. After a few minutes of adjusting his glasses and fidgeting with his napkin, he said, with a sigh, "I may as well begin; I hope you're prepared."

A young man in his thirties, Ian spoke in a quiet voice, with brow furrowed. His good-paying job, he just learned, was coming to a sudden end. It was the last thing he expected. His youngest son just had been diagnosed with a rare form of leukemia, and to top it off, his wife was making noises about divorce, saying she didn't think she loved him anymore!

After telling me all that bad news, Ian went on to say he couldn't sleep, was having great trouble eating, suffered from severe headaches, and was developing an ulcer. He admitted, "I'm worried sick."

Ian isn't alone. Anxiety and high stress are exacting a terrible toll in many people's lives today through divorce, illness, and even suicide. We're moving at breakneck speed. Someone said we're moving so fast these days, we're honking at our own taillights! If our forefathers missed the stage coach to Dodge City, they went back home and waited two weeks for the next one. Today if we miss one turn in the revolving door, we have a nervous breakdown! Or so it seems.

All worry is born out of fear: fear of failure, fear we can't pay our bills, fear of failed health, fear we won't make this deadline or that deadline. People worry about their worries, while others worry over the fact they have no worries when they feel should have some!

Worry takes a toll. It damages health, keeps us from rest, makes us irritable, skews our decisions, and basically prevents us from living the abundant life Jesus came to bring us (John 10:10).

Some unknown author penned these penetrating words about worry:

Some of your hurts you have cured,
The sharpest you still have survived,
But what torments of grief we've endured
Over evils that never arrived.

By far the majority of things we fret, stew, and worry over never happen! I remember so well in the 1950s when fear of nuclear holocaust drove thousands of Americans to build bomb shelters and gather large food stockpiles. Civil defense routes were the talk of the day. Today people worry about the economy. Will I have enough to send my kids to college? Will I be able to pay my mortgage? How will I possibly pay these higher taxes, and how will I afford to retire in a few years with inflation going up and down? If you have suffered from worry, stress, and anxiety, here is some good news for you.

COUNSEL FROM GOD'S WORD

Here are five simple steps to a worry-free life.

I. Understand that worry is futile.

We can't change anything by worrying about it. We can't adjust any circumstance by being anxious over it. Look at the words of Jesus:

"Therefore I tell you, do not worry about your life,
what you will eat or drink; or about your body, what
you will wear. Is not life more important than food,
and the body more important than clothes? Look at the
birds of the air; they do not sow or reap or store away
in barns, and yet your heavenly Father feeds them. Are
you not much more valuable than they? Who of you by
worrying can add a single hour to his life?"
(Matthew 6:25-27).

That last sentence is the clincher! "Who of you by worrying can add a
single hour to his life?" The fact is, by worrying, you may take an hour or two
off your life!

2. Remember worry confirms our distrust of God's sovereignty.

The presence of worry equals the absence of trust in God.

Either God is sovereign over our lives or He isn't. He Himself has said:
"What I have said, that will I bring about; what I have planned, that will I do"
(Isaiah 46:11).

The Lord is fully in control of everything, so for me to worry about anything is to disbelieve what God says in His Word.

One writer put it this way:

Said the robin to the sparrow,
"I would really like to know,
why these anxious human beings
rush around and worry so."
Said the sparrow to the robin:
"Friend, I think that it must be,
they have no heavenly Father
such as cares for you and me."

3. Realize worry and anxiety only lead to evil.

King David had plenty of reasons to worry. Saul was constantly trying to
kill him, and he was on the run most of the time. Yet he wrote:

Do not fret because of evil men or
be envious of those who do wrong....
Be still before the Lord and wait patiently
for him; do not fret when men succeed in
their ways, when they carry out their
wicked schemes" (Psalm 37:1, 7).

Again, David says in that same psalm: "do not fret—it leads only to evil" (Psalm 37:8b). Why? Because when our eyes are off the Lord, we're going to react to circumstances in our flesh, not by His Spirit.

4. Recognize worry itself is sin.

That may sound harsh and legalistic, but it's true. It's not just a human weakness in our life, it's sin. Any command of Scripture we choose to disobey is sin, and Jesus told us: "do not worry" (Matthew 6:31).

Worry is not only sin because it's disobedience, but because it shows a definite absence of trust and faith in a sovereign God. Being anxious is tantamount to saying, "I'm convinced God is not in control of some areas of my life."

The apostle Paul also said, "Do not be anxious about anything" (Philippians 4:6). Notice the word "anything." Paul is saying no situation will ever rear its head in this life that we need to worry about.

5. God has an answer to worry and anxiety.

The first thing God wants us to do is tell Him we're sorry for all our worry and anxiety, and acknowledge we have sinned.

Second, we need to replace worry: "by prayer and petition, with thanksgiving, present your requests to God" (Philippians 4:6).

The result? "The peace of God, which transcends all understanding, will guard your hearts and your minds in Christ Jesus" (Philippians 4:7).

God wants you to take whatever you're worried about, package them up, and pitch them to Him: "Cast all your anxiety on him because he cares for you" (1 Peter 5:7).

If you've been worrying, like Ian, pray this prayer now:

Dear God, I'm truly sorry for all the fretting
and worrying I've done. I acknowledge it to be
sin, and a sign that I'm not trusting you.
I hand over to you right now all that I'm anxious
over, and ask you to do with it what you will.
Help me to be responsible, but not anxious. Amen.

Like Ian, your circumstances may not immediately change. You may still have to deal with specific areas of your life such as adversity, anger, bitterness, or marital difficulties. That's what this book is all about.

But how much better to enjoy God's surpassing peace instead of continuing to worry ourselves sick. Go to God—and His Word—for the counsel you need today!

▪ ▪ ▪ ▪ ▪

More biblical counsel

PSALM 55:22

PSALM 37:4

PSALM 27:1

PSALM 46:1

PSALM 23

PROVERBS 3:5-6

JEREMIAH 29:11

PHILIPPIANS 4:13

PHILIPPIANS 4:19

ROMANS 8:28

How to Choose a Counselor

Many people are at a loss for a criteria that enables them to select a reliable counselor. If after consulting God's Word and wisdom for your particular situation you still feel the need for the help from another person, the following criteria for a good counselor may be of help.

1. A BORN-AGAIN BELIEVER—Be sure this person can tell you that he is eternally saved by God's amazing grace, and how he knows he has eternal life.

2. SPIRITUAL MATURITY—Make sure your selection includes someone whose age and spiritual maturity are adequate to provide resources for you.

3. BIBLICALLY ADEPT—You'll want someone who has more than just a passing knowledge of God's Word. It should be a person committed to the fact that for every problem we face there is a corresponding principle in Scripture to help us through it.

4. COMMITTED TO THE LOCAL CHURCH—Your counselor needs to be a member of a local church, and a supporter of the Bride of Christ. It's perfectly all right to ask about his or her church relationship.

5. COMPLETED TRAINING—Make sure your counselor has had top-quality training in such areas as people skills, relational skills, and of course, the Word of God. Whether your counselor is a lay counselor with no college degree, but with training, or whether he holds a Ph.D., what is important is his ability to see your problem from God's perspective.

6. REFERENCES AVAILABLE—Make sure he or she is willing to provide references that are as recent as one year, and be willing to call the references.

7. REASONABLE REMUNERATION—Some biblical counselors not connected to the local church receive their livelihood from counseling others. Have a clear understanding in the beginning that you are agreeable with the charges or fees, and that they are in line with others in your community.